Thomas Richard Bentley

A Letter to a Member of the House of Commons upon the Meeting

of Parliament

Thomas Richard Bentley

A Letter to a Member of the House of Commons upon the Meeting of Parliament

ISBN/EAN: 9783744764025

Printed in Europe, USA, Canada, Australia, Japan

Cover: Foto ©ninafisch / pixelio.de

More available books at **www.hansebooks.com**

A

LETTER

TO

A Member of the Houfe of Commons,

UPON THE

MEETING OF PARLIAMENT,

BY

THE AUTHOR OF THE LETTERS TO MR. FOX,

UPON THE DANGEROUS AND INFLAMMATORY TENDENCY OF HIS
CONDUCT IN PARLIAMENT,

AND

UPON THE PRINCIPLES, DUTIES, AND COMPOSITION OF MINORITIES.

Ut jam nunc dicat, jam nunc debentia dici,
Pleraque differat et præfens in tempus omittat. Hor.

LONDON:

PRINTED FOR J. OWEN, NO. 168, PICCADILLY.

M DCC XCIV.

ERRATA.

Page 4, Line 2, for contraction, *read* contradiction.
—— 22, — 24, — the unjusteft, *read* their jufteft.
—— 23, — *note*, — in, *read* for.
—— 39, — 29, — dele intereft.
—— 42, — 23, — alteration, *read* alternation.
—— 44, — 23, — it, *read* he.
—— 53, — 15, — whole, *read* noble.
—— 64, — 5, — are, *read* were.
—— 69, — 16, — more, *read* lefs.

A LETTER

TO

A MEMBER OF PARLIAMENT

UPON THE

MEETING OF PARLIAMENT,

&c. &c. &c.

————————

DEAR SIR,

WHEN you engaged me fo anxioufly to put into writing the heads of thofe converfations which I had the pleafure to hold with you, during your ftay at ———, I eafily judged that you were defirous of learning, whether the impreffion they made upon you would be common to other perfons, who could not be biaffed or mifled by that kind and habitual partiality you bear me; when I promifed, therefore, to comply with your wifhes, 'it was with the fecret intention of fubmitting my opinions, not only to fuch of your private friends as you might think proper to confult upon them, but to the Public, which is not, and which has no caufe to be, inclined to think too favourably, in general, of political perfons and of political pretenfions.

In

In fact, Sir, it is but a common juftice to you, that
the fentiments which, I confefs, I have uniformly
endeavoured to inftil into your mind, and the arguments by which I have enforced them, fhould be
fubmitted to an unprejudiced and a difinterefted tribunal; and it is at leaft a great fatisfaction to myfelf
to be able to appeal for its decifion, and to fubmit
to its judgment, whether I have warped your opinions by your affections, and made our friendfhip an
inftrument, inftead of a motive, for perfuading you.
You know I am not of the opinion of Tully, that to
perfect friendfhip it is neceffary to hold the fame political opinions; and, certainly, I think it much lefs
fo at London than it might have been at Rome (to
draw the comparifon between his times and our own)
becaufe there was then no queftion of dividing, and balancing, and tempering the powers and attributes of
Government; and there could exift no parties, but this
of the republic, and that of the ufurpers; it was not
party, but civil war; it was not oppofition, but enmity
and defiance: To range upon the fame fide, therefore,
in difputes like thefe, was undoubtedly neceffary to
the enjoyment, whether it was fo or not to the exiftence of friendfhip. But in our complex and miti-
gated government, the fhades of opinion that form
divifions and parties are fo faint, and frequently fo
metaphyfical, that they are not perceived in the commerce of private life, and can neither obfcure nor
diftinguifh thofe faftidious and affected fects, into
which

which intereft and vanity, rather than either difcord or principle, have fplit and diftributed fociety.

Whether or not, however, this opinion of Cicero be juft, which I doubt; and be applicable, which I deny: I fpeak from my own feelings, which are not unknown to you, when I fay that, his " *idem fentire de republicâ,*" is an apothegm, which has had more fuccefs in the world than it ought to have had, though not more than it might have been eafy to forefee it would obtain, fince it is addreffed more to the paf- fions and the fpleen, than to the virtue or the reafon of mankind; and has too often furnifhed an inge- nious, and at laft a ready and a vulgar excufe for the violation of private ties, obligation, and grati- tude, under that fpecious, but falfe pretext of public principle.

Friendfhip appears to me to be founded entirely upon moral relations; and no difference in political, or even in religious opinions, could, I think, have the power to impair it, unlefs it were already fhaken or decayed in its real foundations. How narrow muft be the foul of him who can forgive no difference?— How bafe the fpirit that can fupport no contradic- tion?—Neither can I admit, excepting as a form of civility, the forrow it is ufual to exprefs, when we differ in opinion from any one. " *Sine verborum con-* " *tumeliâ,*" fays Tully to one of his friends, " *à te* " *diffentire poffum, fine animi fummo dolore non poffum.*"

The

The only effect I can perceive in my own mind, however, to refult from the contraction of my friends is, to make me more doubtful and diffident of my own convictions; it obliges me to analyze my argument, to confider, and enquire, and combine anew my reafons, inferences, and deductions. But all this I can do, I confefs, without experiencing the minuteft fenfation of forrow; or even, what I fufpect to be a more common feeling, of humiliation. For upon what fide of a controverfy is it poffible to range ourfelves, where we fhall not be oppofed by an immenfe authority of opinion? Contradiction therefore, with the permiffion of Cicero, ought to make us uncertain, but not unhappy; to leave us doubtful, but neither mortified nor angry. The oppofition of fentiment in thofe I moft love and efteem, is but an inducement with me to examine the fubject of our difcuffion with increafed accuracy and attention: At the fame time, I acknowledge the ftrong impulfe I feel to convince thofe whom I love and efteem of particular truths, which ought to influence their happinefs or their actions: and that I feel every motive to perfuade them, which friendfhip, or perhaps vanity, can fuggeft to me. Still, if I fail, I am contented with the effort I have made, and am fatisfied that a difference of ideas is not an alienation of our hearts. Had I lived at the beginning of the laft century, when Hampden and Falkland divided the admiration of the age, and had I enjoyed the honourable fortune to be the friend of either, I am fure

I had

I had not ceafed to be fo for the part that either acted upon the theatre of the civil war. Who that feels but a fpark of virtue in his breaft, would have quarrelled with More for his religion, with Sidney or Blake for their politics? Philofophy and party, believe me, can divide none but little minds. I think fometimes, however, that more has been attached to the opinion I am fpeaking of, than can fairly be inferred from it, at leaft if the author of it meant all that is imputed, he has worded it with a more than diplomatic chicanery: and if he had been categorized upon his propofition, he would probably have been driven to defend himfelf by a piece of cafuiftry analogous to what we have heard applauded in a modern Senate, and to have told his opponent, that he meant it as a minifter, but not as a man. With this *diftinguo*, I believe we muft fuffer the axiom to pafs; to which, in effect, no man is fo indifferent as myfelf; for whether it be owing to the particular bias of my own mind, fo totally averfe to all party and to all partizans, or to the conviction I entertain, the refult of the little knowledge I have of hiftory, and of the few obfervations I have made upon mankind, I think party incompatible with all friendfhip, all truth, all fincerity, all honour whatfoever.

In the title-page, you have found me confeffing myfelf the author of two indolent pamphlets, which have occafioned fome difcourfe in the world, and more than once been the fubject of difcuffion be-

tween

tween ourfelves. The fame motives which decided me to with-hold my name from thofe papers, namely, the hurry and inaccuracy with which they were written, will induce me more forcibly to fupprefs it upon the prefent occafion; and I have ftill ftronger reafons, confidering the actual circumftances of the times, to keep my fecret; for I do not pretend, nor flatter myfelf, " *principibus placuiffe viris.*"—I write for you only; though I am content to be read by thofe who, I think, it is but juft fhould determine between us; and it is rather a whimfical, but a real and unaffected coincidence, which makes me acknowledge myfelf to you, and conceal myfelf from all the world befides; though I know not whether it be merely my habitual and incorrigible indolence, or whether I may flatter myfelf that it is a rooted, and conftant contempt of that baftard child of Fame, fo properly called Popularity—Popularity, which mocks or deceives the prefent age, and fets pofterity at defiance. But, befides the neceffity my confeffion fpares me, of recapitulating the arguments contained in thofe infignificant pages, I have another inducement to make it, in the pleafure I feel in bringing back to your recollection the converfations we have held together refpecting them, by which you will be able to call to mind, how very little confident I have ever been in the truth or exactnefs, or anxious in the defence of my own judgment, when placed in oppofition to yours, or even to that of perfons for whom I could not feel all the fame prepoffeffion and deference.

deference. I· shall indulge my vanity at the same time, in making some of those points known to the Public, in which the concurrence of your sentiments has stamped a value upon my own!

A principal point of agreement, as I remember, was the necessity I had argued and enforced, of forming a national party upon a national principle, if we expected either to have any reform in the filth and corruption of our Government, or any security for what is left of independence and liberty; at least if we would avoid obtaining these ends by means fatal to the very being of Parliaments, and to the Constitution itself, by remedies which I have described to be more dangerous, more destructive, than any disease.

Still you considered the unknown author of that opinion as sanguine, and visionary in the extreme, and thought it impossible that his standard could be reared in "*face Romuli*," in the dregs and lees, the sink and kennel of Alfred; or that there could be found a sufficient number of men, pure and uncontaminated enough to desire to repair it. Of the person too, who was openly invited to preside over such a party, you seemed to imagine it particularly unreasonable to form any favourable expectations; and you asserted, that his very appearance in the midst of it would prevent it from being joined by such as would look, no doubt, for a less suspicious and a less violent leader.

Another

Another obfervation of yours I take the liberty of reciting, becaufe I am convinced of its juftice and its force, and have determined to act in conformity with it. The laft of thefe pamphlets, after preffing the Gentleman to whom they are addreffed to reform his party, or rather to form a new one, upon the principles of which I have been fpeaking, feems to promife to point out the means, by which a reform might be accelerated, and the meafures which it would be expedient to purfue in order to obtain it, according to the exifting plan and known hiftory of our conftitution. Here you faid, " There is great " danger of your politician turning projector, and " ftill greater of his caufing his project to mifcarry, " by a premature developement and difclofure of " the whole of it. It will be rejected by many, be- " caufe it *is reform*; by many, becaufe it is *not re-* " *volution;* and he ought to forefee, that it will " pleafe none *perfectly*, but himfelf, and a few of his " partizans."—Whatever, my dear Sir, may be my conviction, with regard to the whole of this opinion of yours, it is perfect with regard to the propriety of with-holding any plan, or project, if that fanciful term become it more, till there fhall appear a bet- ter difpofition to be honeft upon one fide, and to be temperate upon the other; till there fhall arife a fenfe of the fhame and difhonour of with-holding every thing from the people in thofe who owe every thing to the people; and in thofe whofe policy it is to de- mand every thing for the people, a fenfe of the peril

2   and

and the mifchief of obtaining too much, or of obtaining any thing by means of the people; till thofe
who have power fhall perceive 'the danger of denying every thing; and thofe who have popularity, the
wickednefs of grafping and feizing every thing; in
fhort, till there fhall arife a calmer and a wifer fpirit,
a fpirit of juftice on the one hand, and of moderation
on the other, a defire to grant what will otherwife
be exacted, and a difpofition to accept in peace and
tranquillity, what will elfe be the fruit of much un-
happinefs and of many crimes.

I find myfelf under a neceffity, from the confeffion
I have made to you, to vindicate myfelf in another
point, which would, indeed, have been fuperfluous
with regard to yourfelf, but which becomes neceffary
from refpect to the Public, who will naturally lay
the fins of the letter writer to Mr. Fox upon the author of thefe pages, and regard them with the fame
fufpicion which has unfortunately fallen upon the
former. Thofe gentlemen who have been pleafed to
criticife thofe humble performances, in a manner infinitely more favourable than, I doubt, they have
any pretenfions to deferve, have alfo been pleafed to
infinuate a cenfure, which I know it was impoffible
they could have deferved. I have the vanity to think,
Sir, that not only yourfelf, but the whole number
of thofe who are acquainted with their author, if he
had avowed himfelf, would have arifen in refutation

of

of that oblique, but unjuſt accuſation; and that thoſe who made it, if they could have gueſſed or ſuſpected to whom they applied it, would have felt, that no compliment, no flattery to the language and compoſition of his pamphlets, could balance the imputation they have conveyed againſt the principle and the purity of the motive with which they were written.

It has been alledged, that there is an evident variance between the firſt letter and the ſecond; that the firſt, *pour trancher le mot*, is a miniſterial pamphlet; and that the ſecond evidently betrays a miſtruſt, or a diſlike of the Adminiſtration. I ſhall not treſpaſs very long upon your patience in preferring my defence; but to this charge it is neceſſary that I ſhould add the inuendo of my accuſers; they ſay, that as no *Public Event* has happened between the publication of theſe two letters, which could be the cauſe of ſuch a change in opinion, they are afraid the virtue of the writer is not of the pureſt kind.

Now, my dear Sir, I aſſert, in direct contradiction to theſe gentlemen, that the firſt letter was not a miniſterial pamphlet; and that if it had been, a public event had taken place before the writing of the ſefecond, which could have been, and which ought to have been the cauſe of what they call an evident variation; and the dates of theſe two letters are
themſelves

·themfelves the proof it. The firft, written in January, was compofed under the fenfe of the immediate dangers of the country ; and I hope I fhall not
be fufpected of too much vanity, if I venture to
place it by the *State Ballad* of Mr. Bofwell, and call
it a national pamphlet : in fact, it was one, if ever
there was one written or publifhed in any country
under heaven. Threatened with infurrection and revolution at home, with the invafion of our allies,
and with war, both foreign and domeftic, the weak
and paralytic hand of Government had need of every
fuccour, every prop, every fupport. The people ftood
aghaft and terrified, uncertain between the known and
unknown dangers that threatened it. It was neceffary
to ftrengthen the Adminiftration, no matter how,
or of whom it were compofed ; it was neceffary to
induce the nation, diftracted and perplexed with the
impudence and fophiftry of our parties, to confront
its enemies, and to undertake the war with refolution
and with unanimity. In this fpirit was the firft letter
compofed ; with what fuccefs, it is not for me to determine. But were thefe gentlemen at liberty to
infer, that the author was a partizan of Minifters,
becaufe he preffed the declaration of the war, which
has fince been carried into effect ; or that he was in
concert with Government, becaufe he refented the
bafe and malignant artifices of France, and dreaded
the deftruction of our admirable Conftitution at
home ? Were they at liberty to fuppofe, that he approved of *all* their meafures, becaufe he endeavoured. .

to

to encourage and confirm them in *one*, which the honour, the intereft, and the fafety of the country demanded at their hands? Becaufe he expofed the treachery of the *concealed* and the *public* enemy, and endeavoured to with-hold the moft formidable of their
adverfaries from lending hope or authority to the
anarchy which threatened our eftablifhments?—It is
doubtlefs become neceffary for me to proteft againft
conclufions and inferences like thefe;—for me, who
fee no fafety for Europe but in the fuccefs of our
arms; nor for our own liberty and Conftitution, but
in the difmiffion, and punifhment of Minifters, as
foon as we fhall have lefs to dread from their fucceffors than from themfelves........I know thefe fentiments will pleafe no party. Thofe who try to make
a common caufe between the war and corruption,
will not think themfelves obliged to him who defends
the war, but makes war againft corruption; nor be
inclined to pardon the enemy of the Court, in favour
of the defender of the Conftitution. The caufe of
Europe, and the principles of civil fociety, will not
weigh with them againft the cobwebs of the drawing-
room; be'ieve me, the fears they entertain for their
country are not quite equal to their fears for their
falaries.—If thefe perfons will acknowledge no obligation for the little fupport he might have lent to
the Minifter, ftill lefs will the Oppofition, or the
Clubbifts, be inclined to regard, with any partiality
or favour, a writer, whofe virtue, let it be of *what
kind it will*, is certainly not of *their kind*, but detefts
their

their crimes and violence, and deprecates their madnefs and defpair, with fo much appearance, at leaft,
of horror and antipathy, that it has been miftaken
for friendfhip or complicity with the Court! Yet,
Sir, I take my confcience to witnefs, that, though
I have had no party to ferve, no intereft to promote,
no ambition to flatter, I have not written in an idle,
or an unconnected caufe;—I have written to the
wife and moderate of every defcription ; and I have
called on thofe who yet are fullied by no crime nor
bafenefs, who are allied to no proftituted caufe, and
entangled with no dark and intricate engagements,
who have no defire, no intereft, but the welfare and
falvation of their country, who are neither corruption's flaves, nor ambition's dupes ; I have called on
thefe, and I think I have not called in vain ; but I
will call again and again, if I have health and life,
till my voice is heard, and till the fpirit of the country is awake, till public contempt and refentment
brand the profligate factions that rend the State, and
prey upon the commonweal ; till not my voice, but
the voice of the people fhall be heard, and it be unfafe to be wicked ; and dangerous, as well as bafe, to
be publicly unprincipled and corrupt. Behold then
the party to which your friend is attached, to which
he will for ever belong ; and do not think that it is
a creature of his fancy, a chimera of his brain ; believe me, it exifts. The ftatue is yet indeed within
the block, but as it is formed it lives; the Prome-
thean torch has been held to it in the brute rock ;

the

the chiffel gives it fhape and animation at the fame
ftroke ; it affifts itfelf the plaftic hand that feems to
create it, and throws off with the firft effort and curiofity of exiftence the cumbrous cruft that conceals its
fymmetry and proportion. In the mean time

Que puis-je faire de mieux que d'aider de toutes
mes forces à répandre cette vérité *qui prépare les voies?*
On commence par la mal récevoir, peu-à-peu les
efprits s'y accoutument, l'opinion publique fe forme,
& enfin l'on apperçoit *à l'execution*, des principes,
qu'on avait d'abord traités de folles chimeres—dans
prefque tous les ordres des préjugés, fi des ecrivains
n'avoient confenti à paffer pour des fous, le monde
en feroit aujourd'hui moins fage.

But however vifionary or chimerical I may appear
to be in entertaining thefe ideas, the very pamphlet
in queftion is a proof that I cannot hefitate to lend
my little aid and affiftance as often as the country is
in danger—Her peril will always animate my patriotifm ; indifferent to men, and almoft to meafures,
when her fafety or her honour are expofed, I think I
fhall never be afhamed ncr afraid to appear amongft
the foremoft of her defenders; let them belong to
what party they will, or be defcribed by what name
they think proper.

Ειϛ οιωνος αϱιϛος αμυνεϛθαι πεϱι Πατϱης.

And now let me afk, not only of you, my dear Sir,
but of the enlightened and honeft of every party in
the kingdom, whether the month of January, 1793,
when Dumourier had already turned his face towards
Holland, when the decrees of the National Convention had already taken rebellion under the protection
of the victorious armies of France; when London
was deformed and horrible with foreign faces; and
the murderers of Paris and Avignon ftalked fearlefs
through our ftreets; when anarchy and revolution
refounded from every ale-houfe bench ; when rancour and difcontent fcowled from the brows of induftry; when the whole kingdom heaved with
convulfive throes, and the great fabric of our State
trembled upon its bafis ; I fay, let me afk, if that
had been a time to enquire, whether the Minifter
had arrived by wholefome means at the feat of Government, or had prefided there with wifdom or juftice ? Whether it were honeft to have triumphed
over and difhonoured Parliaments, to have broken
his word with the people, to have doubled the corrupt and deftructive influence of the Crown, to have
played, and trimmed, and fpeculated with public
juftice, and polluted with the artifice and fraud of a
politician, the folemn, facred act of a national impeachment * ? Whether it had been a time to difcufs
the

* While the impeachment is pending (if it lafts for another
feven years) I fhall give no opinion that can affect the accufed.
As it concerns the nation and the Houfe of Commons in particular

the juſtice of the plunder of India, the wiſdom of
being cheated by Spain, or the glory of being brow-
beaten by Ruſſia ?

I know

lar, it is intereſting and neceſſary to conſider it ; and I think there
is no time to be loſt ; ſuppoſing too that any arguments of mine
could have weight with the Public, it is incumbent upon me not
to with-hold them. I ſhall certainly not ſay at preſent whether I
think Mr. Haſtings is innocent or guilty. It is ſufficient for me
that he is either one or the other, and that Mr. Pitt, as well as
myſelf, muſt believe him to be either the one or the other. Now,
if he thought Mr. Haſtings guilty, under the articles preferred
againſt him, and that it was incumbent upon the honour and juſtice of the Houſe of Commons, to preſent them at the bar of the
Houſe of Lords, it was his duty to have carried them up with all
the dignity, and all the authority and all the unanimity of the Houſe ;
and inſtead of confiding the impeachment to the conduct of the Oppoſition, a weak party, whom he loſt no opportunity to mortify and
diſcredit, to have aſſumed a principal character himſelf, and to
have named others amongſt the King's ſervants to ſuſtain the parts
it became them to act upon this important ſtage ; it was his duty
to have eſtabliſhed the facts, to have proved the guilt, to have preſ-
ſed the conviction, and to have demanded the puniſhment. There
prevails a ſhrewd ſuſpicion in the country, that if amongſt the
Managers of this proſecution there had appeared either Miniſters
or Crown-Lawyers, or any of the friends of the Chancellor of the
Exchequer, the iſſue, whatever it might have been, would' have
been decided ſome few years paſt, and all thoſe complaints againſt
the indolence, neglect, and faſtidiouſneſs of the Houſe of Peers,
had either never been born, or had been ſtifled as ſoon as they began to cry out. But if Mr. Haſtings had been, in the opinion of
the Chancellor of the Exchequer, a faithful and meritorious ſer-
vant of the Public, I think it was his duty to have defended him
againſt the ſpleen, malevolence, and envy of thoſe who were not
only the enemies of Mr. Haſtings, but his own ; and I think it was

ſo

I know what you will anfwer, and what will be anfwered by all to whom I have appealed; but furely
thofe who are difpofed to judge, or to fpeak fo favourably of me, where I have at beft but very queftionable and imperfect pretenfions, might have recollected, that it had been one of my chief objections to
Mr. Fox, that the conduct of the minority had been
fo abfurd, fo corrupt and unpopular, that it was not
able to refift even the moft defpotic and violent acts
of the adminiftration; that its voice could not be
heard, without contempt, ridicule, and fufpicion;

fo plain a duty, that I know not whether to attribute it to cunning,
to cowardice, or to jealoufy, that he fhould have fhrunk from it.
This point is, however, collateral to the queftion; which ftands
fimply thus; Did he think Mr. Haftings innocent, why fuffer
him to be profecuted? Did he think him guilty; why not caufe
him to be profecuted with all the weight and affiftance of his own
friends, the crown lawyers, and all the authority of the Houfe? Meff.
Burgefs and Rofe, or Rofe and Burgefs, for I know not your
etiquette of precedency, I am told you dabble in politics. What
fay you? Is Haftings guilty? Who difappoints the juftice of the
kingdom? Who defrauds the national procefs of half it dignity?
Who prolongs the wrongs of India, and all the crimes, and all the
fhame of England?—Is Haftings innocent? Who abandons a virtuous minifter to the malice of a party? Who delivers a hero to
feven years of legal perfecution? Speak out, gentlemen; but fpeak
with difcretion. Be fure you do not tell the people of this country,
that the impeachment was connived at, rather than adopted, by minifters, for the purpofe of diverting their attention from the Reform;
or that of digufting them with parliaments altogether. Remember, that unaccountably as Gil Blas came to be fecretary to the
prime minifter, he got, to the full as unexpectedly, into the Tower of
Segovia. Therefore, know your ground, and fpeak from authority.

C · and

and that it was unable to procure the least redrefs, or to refift the greateft oppreffion.

The fecond letter was written, as the date proves, after the expulfion of Dumourier from Holland; after the emancipation of Brabant and Flanders; after all the defeats, and the final defertion of this fantaftical general, whom M. Mallet du Pan compares to Tamerlane the Great. The battles of the Prince of Saxe Cobourg, upon the Maefe and Roer, the recapture of Breda and Gertrudenberg, and the invafion of France, by the victorious armies, might have been confidered, all together, 1 fhould have thought, as a *public event* of fufficient importance not to have been overlooked by the gentlemen who are fo *clair-voyans*, fo ready to fee into *private motives.*

By thefe fucceffes, Sir, in my humble opinion, the whole ftate of affairs was not only changed, but inverted.

Inachias jam venit ad urbes
Dardanus et verfis lugebat Græcia fatis.

France, repreffed within her own frontier, difpirited and enfeebled, by treachery and defeat, could no longer afford any caufe or pretext for immediate apprehenfion; and we had leifure to turn our eyes homewards, and to confider our own domeftic fituation, which had become fo peculiarly interefting and myfterious, by the craft and fraud of one party, and the violence and depravity of another; where

opinion

opinion had been fo artfully fhocked and confounded, and paffions fo wickedly enflamed and ex-
afperated, that we prefented a fpectacle of madnefs
and defperation, of which there is no parallel in the
worft periods of our hiftory. The caufe of liberty
had been coupled with the caufe of France; and the
caufe of corruption confounded with that of Europe
and of civil fociety: The perpetuity of abufes, the
venality of parliaments, the intolerable influence of.
the court, appeared to be defended by the ·gre-
nadiers of Bohemia; while there were men who
looked for reform, and the return of liberty and virtue, from the fucceffes of fuch monfters as Cuftine or
Santerre! The conftitution feemed forgot in the
fquabble; and the policy of the court, affifted by the
violence of the reformers, had fplit the nation into
two factions, in one of which tyranny was the watch-
word, and regicide in the other!

I have more *in petto* to fay upon this fubject; at
prefent I fhall confine myfelf to afk you, whether it
were not become, at this conjuncture, as neceffary to
watch and fufpect the conduct of minifters, as it had
ever been to fupport and invigorate their meafures,
during the dark and dangerous period which pre-
ceded?

I fhall now, my dear Sir, enter at once into my
fubject; *in medias res*; and I take this opportunity to
do fo, becaufe it will feem to be a direct confequence

C 2   deriving

deriving from the depraved and fcandalous ftate of parties in this kingdom, that we fhould either look for one of a purer, honefter, and more popular defcription, to carry our complaints where they muft be heard, and to procure us that redrefs which muft be granted; if we would not expofe our whole fyftem to the violence of thofe, who having right in the beginning, will, of neceffity, become guilty before they leave off. Thofe who teach the people to demand for themfelves, will colour their own ambition with the injuftice and tyranny of thofe who will comply with no other requifitions. Both fides, in my opinion, are criminal; but there is one, which is not only unjuft, but abfurd.

For you, my dear Sir, and a few independent country gentlemen like yourfelf, I am fure you will forgive the good faith and fimplicity with which I fpeak it; for you, and a few good men like yourfelf, to imagine you can direct, or that you can moderate between thefe difcordant parties; that you can reconcile their jarring interefts, or temper their unprincipled and infatiable ambition, is a thought more vain and more vifionary, than what you have objected to the letter-writer. It may be difficult to *form* a pure party, but to attempt to *reform*, or to reftrain parties, inured and difciplined in corruption, or to regulate the exceffes of men who have learned not to blufh, and have left off to feel; who know no paffion but the luft of power; and are excited only by envy and

3   competition :

competition: to pretend to awe, or to govern thofe, whom fuccefs makes bold, and power hardens; or thofe who are become callous or defperate, by difappointment and mortification : I fay, for you to imagine you poffefs this power, is little fhort of the madnefs of him who fhould believe he poffeffed the ring of Solomon, or the lamp of Aladdin.

When you afk me, therefore, whether it be not *neceffary* for an independent member of parliament, who would be of fervice to his country, to give his confidence to one party or the other, in the Houfe of Commons; I anfwer you, that it is *impoffible*; and that it is fo far from being neceffary, that in the actual fituation of parties, the utmoft that you could hope for would be, by ftrengthening fometimes the one, and fometimes the other, to preferve a fpecies of equilibrium between both, and prevent either from being able to accomplifh the complete overthrow of the Conftitution. You will be obliged to imitate *Me*, whom you have blamed, and many others who have not confeffed their fituation ; and to lend your fupport without your confidence, as I have done, and muft continue to do, fo long as the prefent vicious and difgraceful fyftem fhall prevail in our declining empire. Yes, I have written the word, and I will not recall it. A declining empire, difeafed and putrid at the heart; confuming and exhaufting the fprings of life in diftant and violent exertions ; bartering liberty for conqueft, and health for ornament;

drefling

drefling itfelf out like a diftempered whore, in paint, and patches, and finery, while all within is fores, and rags, and rottennefs, and filth, and corruption, and decay.

In advifing you to withold your confidence from either party, I do not counfel you to act an indolent or a negative, no nor a neutral part; neither is it my defire, that you fhould act in a conftant and uniform oppofition to whichever fide might appear likely to gain any momentary fuperiority in the competition. The Oppofition, by denying the juftice, the principle, and the neceffity of the war; and by the indecent and violent means with which it has oppofed it; by the favour it has publifhed towards the caufe of France; and the malignant pleafure, but ill concealed, with which it has regarded our own errors and difgraces; has planted a ftrong and irremoveable barrier between itfelf and the object of its ambition. Whatever its partizans can now fay, will be heard with diftruft and fufpicion; their jufteft reclamations will fall pointlefs upon the ground; their known malevolence will difarm every accufation; their avowed difaffection to the caufe, will be a ftrong challenge againft their cleareft proof and the injufteft conclufion. You will find, and I am not afraid to predict it, that the abfurd and fatal ill conduct and mifcarriages of the war, which will come fo naturally before Parliament, will produce no real effect, no perfect conviction there of the indolence and incapacity of Minifters.

Minifters. You will find, that the inactivity of our
fleets, fo *unaccountable*, or fo *criminal*, will not procure
even the flight and illufory atonement of difplacing
one admiral, or one minifter; that the ignorance and
want of forefight, which has attended our moft fuccefsful operations*, will be detailed and proved, and
even exaggerated in vain; that the want of concert between the troops and the naval forces, deftined to act
againft Dunkirk, and the abfurdity of that undertaking, will all be eafily extenuated, or vanifh before
the greater crimes and turpitude of thofe who will
bring the accufation. And fince I am fo unguard-
edly acting the part of a prophet, give me leave to remark to you, that I am neither new nor unhappy in
that character; I ventured to foretel, that the profligate conduct of Oppofition would render it incapable of deriving any benefit from the miftakes, or ill-
conduct of the Minifters; and this prediction has

---

* At Toulon, though there had been a long negociation between
Lord Hood and the governing people in the town; though Adminiftration will doubtlefs pretend to have planned and forefeen the
furrender of the forts and arfenal; there was not a fingle engineer
officer to take the command of the place. Though not only fuch
an officer, but the neceffary regiments in its defence, ought to have
been fent out, or at leaft embarked at Gibraltar. When I heard
that a very diftinguifhed naval officer was appointed to the command, I afked of another, no lefs fo, whether he confidered himfelf,
or the officer alluded to, to be qualified to defend a fortrefs. He
anfwered me unequivocally in the negative; he could direct the
batteries, but he had no fcience to repair injuries or accidents, or to
defeat the regular approaches of an engineer.

doubtlefs

doubtlefs been realized : for though there is but one fentiment in the kingdom, as far as I am able to dif- cern, refpecting the weak and criminal conduct of affairs; though there is but one opinion with regard to the incapacity, the imbecility, and unfitnefs of the prefent Minifters, to conduct the war, or to negociate with foreign ftates; yet, I do not believe that the fanguine opinion entertained of Mr. Fox's fuperior abilities and vigour in all thefe refpects, has pointed him out to the wifhes of any one thinking or reafon- able man in the kingdom, as a fucceffor to his rival, or fhaken, in the leaft degree, the firm feat of our prefent Adminiftration.

But furely the conduct and fcheme of this war has been as weak and abfurd, as its principle was juft, and its neceffity was evident. Is it not then deplor- able, that this country fhould fee itfelf, by the depra- vity and corruption of the beft and nobleft inftitu- tions, reduced to the dilemma of entrufting the con- duct of its affairs; and abandoning its fleets and armies, the braveft that ever nation owned; its treafure and refources; its fweat and blood; to the caprice and ignorance of one fet of men, or the bad faith and difaffection of another ? That it fhould be obliged to chufe between incapacity and treafon, between abfurdity and ill-will, between folly and malevolence ?

I appeal

I appeal to you, Sir, and to all the world, whether if Mr. Fox had followed the counfels I prefumed to offer him at the beginning of the year; if he had given his fupport to the government, which was ex- pofed, but expofed together with the whole country; if he had difappointed the views and expectations of the factious of every fect and defcription, .by an ho- nourable and unequivocal declaration; if he had pro- claimed the juftice and neceffity of the war, and ex- horted the country to engage in it with refolution and unanimity; if he had refented the injuries and infults offered to it, and the wrongs of Holland, our natural, and *our only natural ally*; I fay I appeal to all the world, whether the miftakes and the mifconduct of his majefty's minifters during one fingle campaign, would not have placed him without any effort, any intrigue, any compromife at the head of affairs? and whether he would not have carried with him into power, a great many perfons who are now combating againft him in both Houfes of Parliament, or ferv- ing his enemies in various departments of the govern- ment, or of the war?

Perhaps, Sir, my fcheme of forming a third party in the country, upon public or national principles, may not by this time appear quite fo romantic, as upon its firft blufh it did to you. For if thofe who admit the juftice and neceffity of the war, but con- demn and lament its ill-conduct, were to rally from every quarter of the kingdom, it is clear that they

could

could not, with any degree of confiftency, or with any reafonable hope of redrefs, affemble round the ftandard either of the Minifter or of Mr. Fox. But had Mr. Fox, whom I invited to become the head of fuch a party, and in conformity to that invitation, to acknowledge the juftice and neceffity of the war; had Mr. Fox hearkened to that advice, it is evident that all thefe perfons would before now have enlifted themfelves under his banners, and as far as the obfer- vation of an individual can extend, and as far as it is reafonable to prefume public opinion, from one's own ftrong but unprejudiced convictions, I am encou- raged to fay, that this would have defcribed five fixths of the property and the talents of the kingdom; that this party would have confifted of every thinking man, not paid by the intolerable wealth and patron- age of the crown, to belong to an exclufive and infu- lated intereft, of every man not corrupted by a profli- gated court, or implicated with a criminal admini- ftration.

But as this gentleman, by a different line of con- duct, has forfeited the confidence, nay even the ear of the country, and as the miftakes, errors, and crimes of his Majefty's fervants, have but too great a chance and probability of efcaping detection, or punifh- ment at leaft, through the contempt and fufpicion into which he and the remnant of his party are fallen, it becomes the duty, as I truft it is yet the privilege of a free and generous fpirit, to prefent thefe grand delinquents

delinquents to the grand jury of the nation, and to convict them before that tribunal, from which neither power, nor greatnefs, nor crowds of mercenary friends can protect them, the tribunal of the public opinion; that high and moral court, whofe cenfure, after that of our private thought, is moft painful, whofe acquittal and applaufe, are the moft dear, the moft honourable enjoyments of life.

When I fpeak of miftakes and crimes, I mean to prove that *both* have been diftinctly committed, not but that miftakes are criminal, and highly criminal, in minifters, particularly a repetition of miftakes; confcious by experience of their folly and incapacity, it is their duty to withdraw and yield the reins of government to a ftronger wrift, and a mightier mind. The foldier is not fhot for being a coward, but the coward is put to death for affuming the character of a foldier. It is not perhaps in our power to be wife or brave, but we are the mafters to refufe a poft where our folly or our cowardice may be fatal to our country.

The firft charge, however, which I fhall bring againft his Majefty's Servants, will not be of a doubtful or equivocal nature; it will be criminal in its fulleft and moft comprehenfive fenfe, and I will prefs it upon the underftanding and confcience of every man in the kingdom, whether it could originate in miftake, incapacity, or folly? and be not the true and legitimate offspring of political intrigue,

of

of patronage, and corruption, or of a corrupt compliance and condefcenfion to the peculiar views and caprice of the court? It will be fcarcely neceffary to point out, that it is the fending of troops to Flanders, and engaging the country in an expenfive and unprofitable war upon the continent, which I prefent as a wilful, corrupt, and deliberate act of delinquency on the part of the King's Minifters; laying my indictment at the feet of the public, and configning it to the memory and archives of the nation, I impeach the King's fervants of this act, as a wilful and premeditated crime; and expecting as I do with ardent vows to heaven, and maturing by every honeft and honourable exertion of my own mind and faculties, that period when juftice may be done once more upon powerful men, in Great Britain, when the purity and integrity of our Conftitution fhall be reftored to us, and when we fhall be freed from the noxious and blafting influence of courts, from the corruption of parliaments, from the torpor, indifference and defpair of the nation; I fay expecting that happy term, I prefer my charge.

I denounce then at the bar of the public opinion, and I take all England, nay the world and pofterity for my judges; I denounce the criminality of the King's Minifters, in engaging the country in a continental war, againft the known interefts and policy of Great-Britain, againft the moft evident convictions, againft the moft conftant experience of the folly, extrava-

gance

gance and danger of fuch a plan! and I affert, that fuch acts are in themfelves criminal, abfolutely and irrelatively to other events, which can only explain or illuftrate the guilt of them, but cannot add to it or increafe it.

Thus, for inftance, though our arms have been difhonoured in the Weft-Indies, though the expeditions againft Martinico and Guadaloupe have mifcarried, for the want of thefe very troops who were mifcarrying from the folly or treachery of Minifters, before the walls of Dunkirk; I fay though our attempts againft the enemy's colonies in that rich weftern Archipelego, which was pointed out by the finger of common fenfe, and of nature herfelf, to recompenfe our maritime and commercial ifland, for the dangers and expences of the war; though our attempts have failed, and our interefts and honour have been facrificed and neglected, all this can add nothing to the pofitive guilt of engaging the kingdom in a continental war; but it is a ftrong and irrefragable proof of the mifchiefs and difgrace which have refulted from that guilty conduct.

The beft Englifhmen and the wifeft politicians, have always dreaded this terrible fcourge, from the connexion of our princes with a German electorate; but fince at length we poffeffed a *native* fovereign, there was reafon to hope that the Englifh intereft might predominate in the councils of St. James's:

The

The paffions, the prejudices of a Britifh King, in favour of his German principality, were no longer likely to warp his Minifters from the plain policy of the country, and to involve a mighty nation in the municipal brawls of the empire. That Hanover fo often preferred to the Englifh diadem, which was fighed for by our kings upon the firft throne of Europe, which we found them regretting, while they held in their hands the umpire and arbitrement of the world,

———*Quem fertur regia Juno*
Pofthabitâ coluiffe famo———

That Hanover, feemed at laft to have found its true weight in the fcale, and the worft danger we had reafonably to apprehend from it, was the giving a foreign education to the younger branches of our royal family, and adding a few more denyzens to the German colony at Pimlico: by what fatality, by what determined treachery, my dear Sir, could it then happen, that without paffions to flatter, or prejudices to comply with, without even that bafe excufe or fubterfuge of deference or fubmiffion to Cæfar, we fhould find ourfelves unexpectedly compromifed, under the firft Britifh prince of the illuftrious family on the throne, and under a Tory Adminiftration, the chief merit of which it hath fometime been, to oppofe and to finifh thefe continental wars; I fay how does it happen that with all thefe circumftances in our favour, we fhould find ourfelves treading back the footfteps of thofe guilty and unfortunate times, when the

spirit

spirit of compliant Whigs devoted our armies on the plains of Fontenoy, or before the ravins of Mount-Caffel!

Will it be pretended that we owed this *good turn* to the Houfe of Auftria, for the diverfion it had cauf-ed in favour of Holland? I acknowledge the fervice, but was the debt fo great, that the gratuitous part we had taken in the war fince the happy accomplifhment of that object, could neither extinguifh nor diminifh it? Could we caufe no diverfion in our turn, with two hundred and eighty veffels of war, which barred, or might have barred, the ports of France, and blockaded her harbours, in the ocean and the Chan-nel, as well as in the Mediterranean? Are our fubfidies, our ftores nothing? Are not they to be counted to-wards balancing this mighty debt to Auftria? Are the ftipendiary forces of Piedmont and Savoy nothing? Are our contracts with Heffe and Hanover nothing? Is the King of Pruffia preferved to the alliance by the weight and intereft, and I fear the treafure of England nothing? Are Florence, Genoa, coerced by the terror of our Fleets, are the manifeftos of Mr. Drake and my Lord Hervey nothing? Oh, fentiment divine of gratitude fo rare in the bofom of ftatefmen, fo new in the hiftory of nations!—Oh, amiable Court of Saint James's! Oh, fortunate Chancery of Vienna!

Oh debt immenfe of endlefs gratitude,
So burdenfome, ftill paying, ftill to owe!

But

But I fear, Sir, and I am compelled in candour to confefs my fear, that the relief of Maeftricht and the victories of Monfieur de Cobourg, are not the only obligations we may be held to lie under to the Houfe of Auftria; or at leaft that if we have no further obligations to acquit, we have errors to repair, and injuries to expiate! I fear that the failure of the fiege of Maubeuge is carried to the debtor fide of the account, and that the bill is fwelled not only by our fatal obftinacy in dividing the allied forces, to undertake that of Dunkirk, but by the-critical affiftance we received after our misfortunes before it. The main body of the army extended its incurfions from Quefnoy to the gates of Peronne and St. Quentin's, and might have fat down before Maubeuge or Cambrai, but was compelled to a virtual inactivity, while no contemptible portion of its force was led through the enemy's country from Valenciennes to Dunkirk, along the fortified roads and intrenched pofts of the French, fatigued and diminifhed by continual and ufelefs fkirmifhes, taking villages by ftorm, blockading farms, and invefting parifhes. While Tournay and Courtray offered a fecure march, and the army would have arrived by a route fcarce at all circuitous, and free from every obftacle and danger, fooner and unimpaired in the country where it was deftined to act *.

* After the taking of Valenciennes, in confequence of a long march and fuccefsful movements, the enemy retiring every way before it, Maubeuge became blockaded; the Duke of York was at Orchies,

from

But when the Britifh army arrived at Dunkirk, I muft afk of the moft determined partizan of government, whether fuppofing the policy of that unfortunate expedition, and the policy of not only weakening but offending Monfieur de Saxe-Cobourg, I muft afk of him whether it were politic too, that there fhould exift no concert nor underftanding between the Board of Admiralty and the Board of Ordnance, and between neither of thefe and the army? Whether it were politic that the gun-boats and battering veffels fhould have been conftructing at Woolwich when they ought to have been in the channel, and the balls yet uncaft at Carron which were deftined to level the Ramparts of Dunkirk ?*

from whence the army began its march on the 15th of Auguft, through Cifoin, and Lannoy, near which places it encamped on the fucceffive evenings, the next day it arrived at Menin, near which it croffed the Lys on Pontons. In the evening the guards repaffed the Lys at Menin, (the bridge of Pontons having been removed) for Lincelles.

* The author of this letter, for obvious reafons, cannot pledge himfelf to *prove* this fact. He however afferts it upon his own perfect knowledge, and he defies the King's fervants, and the Mafter General of· the Ordnance in particular, to *difprove* it. When there came an order to the Warren for 80,000 balls, there was not half that number in this great arfenal of the kingdom—the fhips of war were obliged to fail without their complete armament, and amongft the crews of feveral fhips of the line, there was not a fingle cutlafs. Fortunately the Nymphe was not amongft this clafs or number. He afferts this fact with the *fame* defiance !

D   Let

Let me afk too, I care not of whom, for all the
wealth of the treafury could not buy, nor all the impudence of party fupply more than one anfwer,
whether fuppofing the policy of a continental war, it
were politic too to difcourage and difpirit our brave
troops, by the moft dreadful fpecies of negleſt in the
provifion of the hofpitals, in the choice of the Sur-
geons? Profufion has reigned in every other department, but it remains to be proved, that avarice and
parfimony were the caufes of the deficiency in this—
The drugs were of the worft quality, though the
quantity was an impediment to the movement of the
hofpitals, and is in itfelf a proper objeſt of public enquiry, and fcarcely one man in ten who was fent out
knew the nature of a gun fhot wound—The number
of brave-fellows who have fallen victims to their ignorance, is a fubjeſt upon which the callous minds
of Minifters can fcarce think with indifference. The
wounded officers have all had leave to come home, the
poor privates, alas, could not meet with this indulgence,
' *Animæ viles inhumata infletaque turba !*' But the voice
of humanity, but the national honour and charaſter,
will furely provoke a parliamentary enquiry. Mr.
Hunter is no more, or he might in his own vindica-
tion have condefcended to inform us, by what job the
recommendation to thefe appointments was feparated
from his office, or by what cafuiftry he could defend
it to his confcience or the country, to have given a
diploma to a parcel of raw Scots lads, to maim, and
mutilate, and murder the Britifh troops, becaufe of

their

their intereſt in a burgh or a corporation ? He might perhaps have told the public how many of theſe ſurgeons or their mates, he had appointed, and whether they paſſed their examination before him or the clerks in the treaſury ?

Ευλυχυς ιατρους, οτι τας μιν επιλυχιας ο Ηλιος ορα, τας δὲ απολυχιας η Γη καλυπτει.

While the ſolicitude of Miniſters was divided between Flanders and their villas, while they ſcoured through the country, now to councils and now to dinners, purſued by couriers ſometimes, and ſometimes by admirals and commanders in chief, the aſtoniſhed kingdom beheld with mixed indignation and gratitude, our Weſt-India fleet laden with five millions of property at the leaſt, bringing·an aid of a million ſterling to the revenue, and two thouſand of our beſt and braveſt ſeamen, to man the royal navy ; I ſay it beheld with mixed ſentiments of gratitude and indignation, our invaluable merchantmen enter the channel under the protection of *an eight and twenty gun frigate.* Aſhamed of the diſgraceful danger we had run, we ſcarce dared to be thankful, frightened even at our unmerited eſcape we were too proud to rejoice, with a ſullen but an honourable ſilence we received this boon of heaven, which had wafted our argoſies, through the fleets and cruiſers of our enemy into our own ports, with no convoy but fortune, no admiral but Providence !

Give

Give me leave to paufe for a moment here, not to comment upon the crime, but to withdraw my eyes from a fpectacle fo hideous, fo full of fear and dif-honour—our heads grow giddy when we look calmly down from the precipice, from which an accident or a miracle has preferved us.

And now let me afk you, my dear Sir, who poffefs as much good fenfe, and as much candour alfo, as any man exifting, of you who have an opinion and a vote to give in this extraordinary trial, of you by whom other men, I fpeak not merely of your friends or your conftituents, by whom other men, who know your independence and your integrity, and who place confidence in your abilities and difcernment, may regulate their own opinions and conduct; let me afk of you whether it be poffible, I mean confif-tently with our public duties, to overlook all this neglect and fupinenefs, or to excufe the criminal plan laid down in the cabinet for the conduct of the war, and the abfurd and defective execution of that criminal plan by the feveral boards and departments of Government? Let me afk of you, whether it be a fufficient fatisfaction and atonement to the people of thefe kingdoms to difplace an odious minifter, or an ill tempered admiral, or to fix the *unpunifhed* guilt upon the Admiralty, or the Ordnance? That the Firft Lord of the Admiralty, and the Comman-der in Chief of the naval forces of Great Britain def-pife and deteft each other, is no fecret to the country

at

at large, and the country at large is very willing to range upon either, or upon both sides of so just a dispute. To turn out the Duke of Richmond may gratify the spleen, envy, and ill-nature of ministers, and coincide, in some degree, with the wishes of the nation; to force my Lord Chatham to decide between the Admiralty Board, where his apparition is a phœnomenon, and White's Club, where his absence would be considered as a fearful omen of public misfortune, might lull the public complaints and anxiety for one day, but could not, nor ought to do it for a second. Still it is singular that every accusation is dropped, and all animosity extinguished; for it is not here, " *duo si discordia vexat inertes :*" Tacitus has an expression somewhere, which describes the case with greater truth and precision—" *Conscientia criminis,* says he, *pro amicitia est :*"—To be in a common fault is a species of friendship; (you see I translate for the Attorney-General). After what I have said, and, I trust, after what you know of my disposition, you will not think me particularly anxious to require the immediate dismission or punishment of any of the King's servants; though, were I consulted, I should feel myself obliged to advise it. But I cannot help being somewhat surprized, that such a measure has not been judged prudent and political, considering the great disappointment of the public expectation, and the miscarriage and disgrace which has attended so many of our expeditions. Indeed, Sir, I am of opinion, that the root lies deep and branches

wide,

wide, which enables Adminiſtration to fit ſo firm, and to feel ſo ſecure, under ſo great a weight of political diſcontent and diſappointment; and I ſuſpeƈt, that any family, which can ſo far brave and deride the public opinion, muſt be grown ſomewhat too powerful, bothfor the ſafety of the country and its own!

If we were to throw our eye together over the compoſition of the Cabinet, I think we ſhould find matter not only for aſtoniſhment but for alarm: At the head of all, the Miniſter, his brother preſiding over the Admiralty; his couſin one Secretary of State, his creature the other! To preſerve any kind of equilibrium or counterpoiſe to this enormous weight, fatigues the policy, and exhauſts the genius of the Court: The balance of Europe never employed ſo much thought, cabal, and intrigue, as the balance of the Cabinet of Saint James's. For this Lord Hawkeſbury watches and trembles; for this all colour has forſworne his cheek, and the pen ſhakes in his indefatigable fingers! But it is not here alone that the miniſterial family ſeems to have obtained an undue preponderance; we might contemplate it in another point of view, where it ſeems to hold the compliant conſcience of Parliament; and threatening now reform, and now diſſolution, is as powerful at Weſtminſter, as it is ſuſpeƈted, or formidable at St. James's. Shall we ſtrengthen this ambitious Houſe, which is new to the country? Are we certain that we ſhould not entail a private deſpo-

nobly;

tifm over the Crown and the Houfe of Commons ?
I am fure you think too juftly, too honeftly, too
nobly ; you have family, you have property in the
kingdom ; you have a ftake too great, both in mind
and body, to be committed to adventurers. If we
were to examine the conduct of affairs fince they took
poffeffion of the helm, what promife have they kept
with the people, what right have they reftored, what
advantage have they obtained for it ? We will not
rake the cinders of Oczacow; we will not purfue
them too Nootka-Sound ; hiftory, pofterity will
judge them, and with them that pernicious and dif-
honourable principle, that it is permitted to arm
where it is not permitted to go to war, and that a
generous and mighty nation may threaten where it
dares not, or cannot fight,

Habitet fecum & fit pectore in illo.

Neither will I lead you, for the prefent at leaft, to
examine into the artifice and duplicity which mifcarried in the Commercial Treaty with Ireland, nor
the undifguifed fraud and impudence which made the
Declaratory Bill fuccefsful in Great-Britain. The
prodigality with which the favours of the Crown have
been lavifhed, and the malignity with which the
hopes or pretenfions of particular families, too proud
or too honeft to worfhip the political idol of the day,
have been difappointed. The creation of new orders
of *exploded chivalry*, and the extenfion of the moft
honourable and diftinguifhed of the old intereft, I
have already flightly remarked in the letters to which

D 3   I have

I have alluded. It is true, the crime and turpitude
of all thefe things is more than doubled by the info-
lence and mockery with which they are perpetrated,
at a period of time when Parliaments have declared
the neceffity of abolifhing the influence of the Crown;
and the Minifters of the Crown, the neceffity of fetting bounds to the corruption of Parliaments ! And
it is true too, that thofe perfons who have accufed
the Minifter with having adopted the dangerous and
ungrateful policy of degrading and difhonouring Parliaments, and reducing them to be the mere inftruments and regifters of the will of the Court, have derived an unexpected ftrength to their arguments from
the oftentation with which prodigality has been an-
nounced, and the impudence with which it has been
defended. And though thefe perfons will, it is to
be hoped, find fome difficulty in procuring profelytes to their opinion, it would be uncandid in us,
not to acknowledge, that it would have been eafier
to repel their charge; if the vice and corruption of
the Houfe of Commons had not been expofed with
fo much acrimony, and fo much addrefs by the Minifter himfelf; if it had not been violently diffolved
and humiliated in 1784, and encouraged and incited
from that period to the prefent, to fet the petitions
for reform at defiance, and to deny to the prayers of
the people the abolition of a fingle dilapidated bo-
rough !

Nothing

Nothing appears to me fo dangerous in public affairs, as to leave accufations, no matter how falfe or improbable, if they are attended with a fpecies of plaufibility, unanfwered and unrefuted; becaufe the family of Accufations is not only prolific, but multipaous; and becaufe, notwithftanding their ferpent origin, they do not always rife to deftroy one another, but fometimes unite and embrace, and defend and promote one another, with all the zeal and adhe renceof Scotch confanguinity and connection.— Let us return to the Cabinet.

I do not only fufpect, as I have already expreffed to you, that a certain Houfe may be grown too powerful; in confequence of which, it may not only appear fafe to pardon, or to overlook particular acts of negligence and delinquency, but unfafe to punifh or to difmifs, or in any fhape to vary, or diſturb the nice equilibrium of the balance. But I fear, and I more than fear, for I am convinced of it, and confirmed in it, by my obfervation, and converfation with other perfons, more able to judge and determine, in fuch a matter, than I can pretend to be, that the King's fervants deceive themfelves, and miftake the ground they ftand upon in the public opinion; an error the more eafy, and not the lefs fatal, for them to fall into, fince the terror held out to the public opinion, by the feverity of fome late profecutions and punifhments. Certainly, my dear Sir, if the fears of one fide of the prefs, or the profligacy

of

of the other, have induced the King's fervants to
confider the diftruft and diflike we bear to fome of
thofe who oppofe them, as confidence or affection towards themfelves; if they vainly and falfely interpret
our averfion to anarchy and revolutions, into any
approbation of their own conduct or maxims of Government; if they will not diftinguifh between our
juft hatred of others and our juft fufpicion of themfelves, between our *conflernation* and *forrow* at their
own ignorance and imbecility, and our greater dread
of the principles and defigns of thofe who poffefs
more vigour and ability; I fay, Sir, if they are lul-
led by the delufions of felf-love and vanity into this
fond belief, it is to be feared their errors cannot long
remain undetected, nor be finally difcovered, without fome fatal prejudice to the peace and tranquillity of the nation. For though it is difficult to fore ·
fee, or at leaft would be vain and confident to declare, with precifion, the period of any delufion, it
is not only fafe, but it is modeft to affert, that the
people cannot for ever confent or fubmit to be guided
through the wildernefs of our prefent politics by this
pillar of fmoke, which knows no alteration of light;
and that, fatigued with its wanderings, and fick of
its diet, it will demand other leaders, or, perhaps,
other Gods. ˙.

The terror of French examples, and the hatred of
French principles, have been artfully excited and
encouraged by the partizans of Minifters; I fay artfully

fully, not becaufe it has been done unjuftly, but be caufe it has been done with defign; the cry of " Jacobin, Jacobin," has been bellowed fo loudly in our ears, that we have grown at laft deaf to it, juft as thofe who make it, fhut their eyes while they make it, that they may roar the louder. But this cry would not have echoed fo conftantly to our organs, the minifterial tocfin would not have rung fo uninterruptedly in every parifh of the kingdom, for the fole purpofe of exciting our deteftation of the crimes and maffacres that were committing in France! Thank God, there was no neceffity to imbue the minds of Englifhmen with hatred, and with horror, againft murderers, and the murderers of women and of Kings. The example of France too had ceafed to be dangerous as foon as ever her arms became fo. Since the 10th of Auguft, or the 30th of September at lateft, in the year 1792, Europe has not been exposed to the danger of being corrupted, but of being conquered by the Republic; fhe has not been exposed to be deluded, but to be over-run; fhe has not been threatened with fophifms and paradoxes, but with bayonets and canon; fhe is not invaded by feditious principles and revolutionary writings, but by barbarous hordes, which mifery vomits from their native land, which defpair, a moral, and hunger a phyfical neceffity, compell to conquer, and their adopted principles to defolate mankind. No, Sir, the cry fo artfully encouraged and prolonged, was prolonged at leaft, to anfwer the purpofes of party

and

and of corruption at home. The Jacobins, who were reprefented in fuch odious colours, and pointed out to fo much fufpicion and perfecution, were not always thofe who had put all the property, and all the lives in France, under a conftant ftate of requi-fition, and lined her extended frontiers with armed peafants, compelled to march from her center; it was not always the Jacobins who threatened, and who threaten ftill to deluge Europe with their *na-tionality* and their pikes; but the Jacobins, who wifhed to reform the abufes of the Court, and fecure the liberty and independency of Parliaments; the Jacobins, who would have been worfhipped at the Revolution, and who threatened to reftore the con-ftitution to the principles which prevailed, or were recognized at the Revolution. Thefe were more terrible to our placemen and courtiers, than the Ja-cobins, that were deftroying the very principle of property, and levelling every hedge, and removing every land-mark in Europe. Could there have been at fuch a time, and during fcenes like the prefent, an indifferent fpectator in any part of our trembling quarter of the globe, it muft have fmiled to obferve the vigilance and activity of the war which had been declared againft the bookfellers, while that which was waged againft the Republic, feemed liable to all the demurrers and interlocutors of a Court of Chancery; he would have contrafted the vigour of the crown-lawyers, and their victories too, with the caution of our Admirals, and with their mifcarriages;

he

he would have compared the manifeftoes of the Attorney-General with the informations of the Minifter; and I fear, Sir, he would have more than fmiled,
to contemplate the triumphs of Government, atchiev-
ed, not by our fleets and armies, but by our juftices
and juries, our prifons more filled with printers than
with Frenchmen, and the circuits fo much more glorious and fuccefsful than the campaign! I will not
indulge the pleafantry that fuggefts itfelf unwillingly
to my mind; unwillingly, indeed, for it is in fpite
of our misfortunes and difhonour.—To return.

There certainly was no longer any danger of our
imitating the French Revolution. France might ftill
preach, indeed; but emaciated and expiring in her bath
of blood, with all her fcribes around her, fhe did not
prefent fo lovely a picture to the eye, nor addrefs
fuch winning fentences to the ear or heart, that we
needed to dread the influence either of her precepts
or her example. But what at firft fight feems unaccountable, the danger that had fucceeded to this was
at leaft as carefully concealed and diffembled by the
Court and the Cabinet, as ever the preceding ones
had been by the Oppofition, or the Reformers. A
learned Gentleman has written a very laborious pamphlet (I mean laborious to read, for I think too well
of his talents to fufpect he found any great difficulty
in the compofition) for the purpofe of explaining to
us the " real grounds of the war." But with the
leave of the learned Gentleman, (" *quem dii donent
tonfore*," may he foon be a Serjeant) he has confounded

founded the grounds of the war with the circum-
ſtances that made it impoſſible to delay hoſtilities beyond the month of February, 1793. It is not an
information nor an indictment againſt the National
Convention, that it ſhould have been required of
the learned Gentleman's induſtry to draw up, it is
not an accuſation againſt thoſe who are already condemned, nor is it a cold enumeration of their various
follies and delinquencies that could have juſtified the
enormous promiſe of his title-page. I expected, I
confeſs, when I took up his pamphlet, that he would
have told us what were the cauſes of the war, which
had not yet been avowed by his majeſty's ſervants ;
or, at leaſt, that he would have defended and eſtabliſhed all thoſe which they had hitherto aſſigned for
it. To ſay the truth, I was at leaſt diſappointed, but
the learned Gentleman ſhall experience no aſperity
from me. When I find, in the month of November his Majeſty's Miniſters publiſhing· THEIR
" REAL GROUNDS OF THE WAR," and find theſe
grounds concealed and diſſembled in the Royal Ma-
nifeſto, it would be unpardonable, indeed, not to
pardon JOHN BOWLES ESQUIRE ! But it would be,
I think, more unpardonable; nay, I think it were
an act of cowardice or treachery to ſuppreſs one's feelings, upon all this baſe and diſhonourable chicanery.
Thoſe who arrogate to themſelves to ſpeak in a nation's name, ſhould at leaſt be capable of aſſuming,
for a moment, the national character and ſincerity.
They ſhould diſtinguiſh between their habitual diſ-

ſimulation

fimulation and falfehood as Minifters, and thofe pe-
riodical acts.of ftate, which are authenticated and
impreffed with the characters of truth by name or
fignature of the Sovereign! The real ground of
this war is to repel invafion, to refift oppreffion, to
defend the laws, the liberty, the religion, the hearths,
the fields, of Great Britain ; the grond of the war is
the ground we ftand upon ; itis our native foil, upon.
which we rear our children, which hides the dear and
facred remains of our beloved progenitors ! Let me
refume myfelf—What is it we are fighting for ? for
the ancient Monarchy in France ? Heaven forbid !
For the Conftitutional Monarchy and the Jacobins
of 1789, as vile and criminal, though not fo able, or
fo bold as thofe of 1792 ? Still Heaven forbid ! To
deftroy the Republic under any pretence? Oh, Heaven forbid ! Why then have we combined all Europe in a common caufe ? And why do we cover
the ocean with our fleets, and the continent with our
tents ? To comprefs within the girdle of their ftate,
a ferocious race, who have declared an interneciary
war, againft every eftablifhment, every form of human polity, every order of civil life and fociety ; who
have trampled upon every tye, every duty, every
principle which connects men together, who have
broke through every attachment, either local, or natural, or civil, who have made all property common,
and put the perfons, the property, the profeffions,
and the will of men at the public requifition ? Who
fweep with indifcriminating fury, the inhabitants
                                                    from

from the villages, and drive their peafants from the plough to the flaughter-houfe, indifferent to their loffes, impenetrable to pity or remorfe; a race, who have forfworn commerce and the peaceful arts, who have left their fields unfown, while they meditate the plunder of foreign harvefts; who have left their houfes defolate and forlorn, while they threaten with conqueft and extermination, the towns, the farms, the cottages of furrounding nations.

Thefe are the caufes of the war, and the caufes too why all the queftions that regard a peace are fo vain and illufory? Why fhould we treat (I fpeak not now of the national character and glory) why fhould we treat? Will treaties bind this furious people? No: they muft perceive their own madnefs, and punifh their own criminals before any power can treat with them; and they muft return to principles, and to arts, and employments too, before we or other ftates can lay down our arms with fecurity. We cannot make peace, becaufe if we made peace, they would only be the more intent and the more powerful to make war; but it is fingular that the King's Servants, who I am not afraid to affirm, deferve every punifhment, if they make the war or would make the peace upon different principles, fhould preferve the filence and difcretion of their advocate, fince one would naturally imagine their caufe would derive credit and popularity from the carefull and elaborate difplay, either he or themfelves are fo well calculated to

make

make of them. But when the conduct of the war is
fo criminal, and fo unfortunate, there is fome policy,
or rather cunning, I think, in diffembling the importance of the ftake. I fubmit to you, Sir, whether
even this act of bafenefs and duplicity, could have
been fafely put in practice, without a greater degree
of power and fecurity than any one family ought to
feel or to poffefs?

I appeal, therefore, to you once more, whether it
be poffible to give confidence (I fpeak not now of
fupport, but believe me, it is a terrible fituation,
both for the country, and for the peace and confcience of individuals, to be obliged to feparate confidence from fupport) to give confidence to one im-
perious family, or to one overbearing Minifter, who
either knows not, or conceals the political ftate of
Europe, and of the kingdom; who having conquered Parliament, is enabled to brave and defy the People; who having publicly broken his word with the
People, has entrenched himfelf behind a hedge of
parliamentry corruption, of titles, places, penfions,
and ribbands, till he fits fecure of punifhment, and
impenetrable to fhame?

Oh fi tefticuli vena ulla paterni
Viveret in nobis!

" We are fo far," fays my Lord Bolingbroke, in
fome part of his political writings, " from poffeffing
the virtues of our anceftors, that we have not inhe-

E   This

rited even the fpirit and manlinefs of their vices."
This was no doubt addreffed to the feelings of thofe
whom the proftituted Minifter of his time had corrupted, or whom corruption enabled the Minifter
to infult and fet at defiance. What would that ardent fpirit, that eloquent tongue, have faid to us, had
he furvived into our time, and beheld all the vices,
all the corruption of Walpole, near the throne ; without his love for the Conftitution, his good-nature, or
fincerity ?* What would he have faid, if inftead of

---

* The prefs was never more free than under Sir Robert Walpole's Adminiftration. He engaged mercenary writers it is true,
but not with more tafte or difcernment, nor to a greater extent,
than is actually practifed by Government : the field, however, was
open to his antagonifts ; and during the whole period of his power
the defpotifm of informations, and the fervility of Attornies and
Solicitors General were never directed, as they have fince been, to
crufh the liberty of opinion, and ftifle the very murmurs of liberty.

Unlike to fome of his fucceffors, this man was not *nulla virtute
redemptus a vitiis*; he poffeffed fome of the fterling virtues of the
country, though they were frequently extinguifhed or obfcured by
the vices of his fituation : he was not a hypocrite even in corruption ; and though he was enough a Minifter to bribe, he was too
much an Englifhman to opprefs. He loved peace, becaufe he
thought it was neceffary to the commerce and profperity of his
country : if he fubfidized the electors of the empire, or the
kings of the north, it was to preferve peace, and to gratify,
without the expence, and the calamities of war, that German
Στοργη which he found to be uncontroulable in the Princes on
the throne. His vices were prominent from the blunt Englifh fincerity of his character ; and even thefe may be regretted in England as often as his virtues fhall be wanting in fucceffors, who fhall
poffefs and exceed them all ; and whenever the hypocrites and pha-
rifees

his brother Horace, patient, vigilant, indefatigable in bufinefs, he had beheld a brother, negligent, ignorant, indolent, inacceffible, prefiding over the very firft active department in the war, but invifible to an officer, and a ftranger at his own board? What if the foreign feals in the hands of another relation, pufhed up to premature honours, and the counterpart, in vanity and inexperience, to his coufin? *Oh generis fiducia!* What if another Minifter, whom it would be a libel to defcribe by any thing but his offices, holding the fceptre of India in one hand, and the Secretary's feals in the other, enthroned in Leadenhall-ftreet, and cringing at St. James's; prefiding befides over another board of equal emolument, and almoft equal importance, not to mention I know not how many offices and finecures in Scotland? What if he difcovered another Scotfman at the head of the Court of Chancery,* forming a party under

rifees of Adminiftration fhall offer profane and oftentatious thanks in the Temple, that they are not as this Publican!

* It may be thought I have faid little of this important profelyte, and it may be attributed to faftidioufnefs. But I caution the public againft drawing fuch an inference from my referve. I proteft I refpect my Lord Loughborough as much, I think, as any of his Majefty's Minifters; and I deem him, in many refpects, a fit perfon to prefide over the Court of Chancery. As to his being a Scotfman, it is doubtlefs his misfortune; but I think the objection would have come better when Rome was Rome, while we could have punifhed the treacheries of our Alban neighbour

or

under the patronage and connivance of a man, whether he be a Minifter or not, I defy any one to tell
me: a King's friend (as if Kings had friends) a King's
favourite, the eye-fore of every Adminiftration, the
enemy and the accomplice of every Minifter : cold,
cowardly, and callous, intriguing, plotting, balancing, undermining, overthrowing every man and every
fyftem by turns; too bafe and timid to truft himfelf
in the noon and glare of power, fhrinking and
creeping in the rank fhade and thicket of favour;
like the baleful ivy that climbs and tangles round our
royal oak, blafting the noble pith with its chill gratitude, blighting the verdant arms with its accurft
embraces? What, I fay, if he faw fuch a man providing refources and palliatives, applying his *orvietan*
or *catholicon*, his political noftrums and quackeries,

or at leaft defpifed them, with a found confcience, and with un-
wrung withers; and while it was of confequence to our feelings of
honour, as well as to our interefts, who were the guardians of our
rights, and the oracles of our laws; before it had been dreamed that
courts of judicature might become inftruments of minifterial
revenge or policy; and while there feemed no lefs reafon to dread
unjuft decifions between man and man, than between the fubject
and the crown. For my own part, I am happy to fee this noble
lawyer placed where his fentences can neither be liable to the fufpicion nor the temptation of complacency to the Court. And I rejoice, in the prefent crifis of affairs, not only to behold him where
he is, but to mifs him where he is no longer. I will not weigh a
hundred Dunkirks (a town, by the bye, not unapt to prove fatal to
Chancellors) nor the expence of providing for all his clan at Toulon, nor all the falaries, the half-pay, and the penfions that untenable town ftill cofts us, againft the purity, the unfpotted character
of one court of common law!

to protect the Crown against its own servant; forming subdivisions of parties, and subdividing these, marshalling Court Lords, and instructing Court Members, appointing Chancellors, and Presidents, and Privy Seals; and all to protect the King against the overbearing influence of his own Minister? Ah, what would he not have said? He would have shaken our astonished souls; his patriot accents would have quivered in our degenerate hearts, would have roused the Briton-part of us, the *Divinæ particulam auræ*.

Oh, Bolingbroke! thou hadst not founded a trumpet in a deaf man's ear! Truth, the necessity of thy soul; Virtue, the genius of thy birth; and Honour, the nurse and Mentor of thy whole nature; all had spoken to us in thee! Thy lips, where Eloquence, where Conviction sate; thy classic lips, whence Reason and Persuasion flowed in mingling streams; thy ardent spirit, and thy tongue of fire, had broke the sleep of slaves, and stung the souls of tyrants! St. John, awake! break through thy Runic slumber: reach me thy pen of flame, to which the fall of hypocrites and traitors is promised and reserved by Fate! Or rather come thou, like some heaven-favoured hero, to dispel the mist that hangs upon our eyes, and hangs upon our souls! Come, and dispel the charms of that accurst enchantress, that Circæan hag, CORRUPTION! CORRUPTION! that deforms our character, depraves our mind, and brutalizes our

E 3   existence!

exiftence! Bid us be men once more; the nobleft
of the race of men, be Britons!

It is very natural, my dear Sir, and I had the pleafure to find you fully fenfible of the importance of
the obfervation, to confider the relative weaknefs of
Miniftry, at a time when there is hardly any vifible
oppofition to it in Parliament; and when that oppofition is become both hateful and contemptible in
the eyes of the nation. The fears and artifices of
Government too, are fo much the more worthy of our
attention at the prefent moment, becaufe its pofitive
ftrength is fo enormoufly preponderant, that it is
evident there muft exift fome fecret moral counter-
poife to fo great a phyfical inequality. When we
contemplate an Adminiftration fo powerful, as I think
has no parallel in the free hiftory of our country,
ftrengthened not only by numerous and important
defertions, but by the common apprehenfion and
danger of all the proprietors in the kingdom; I fay,
when we fee fuch an Adminiftration trembling and
wavering, and wanting courage to announce to us all
the real dangers that furround us, it is clear either
that it is itfelf confcious of its own incapacity and
inability to extricate us from them, and of errors and
crimes committed by it, of which the fatal confequences can be only concealed by diffembling the
perilous fituation of the country: or elfe that it is itfelf
curbed and preffed down by the weight of fome fuperior, but invifible power. Another circumftance,
which

which I think well worthy your reflection, is the great
degree of caution with which, notwithstanding all
their antipathy to Jacobins and Republicans, the
King's fervants have avoided to pledge themfelves
againft treating with the French regicides. Even
the declaration of my Lord Auckland, before they
would affume its defence, was emafculated in the
tranflation, with an affected ignorance of the French
language, and a wilful violation of one of the com-
moneft of its idioms. Now, Sir, why all this anxiety
in Minifters to keep fome poftern for negociation,
fome pretence in referve, fome hope or contingency
for treating ? *Ufque adeone mori miferum eft ?* Are they
determined in cafe of final difcomfiture and humiliation, to treat with the Jacobins rather than refign ?
When they have ruined us by the war, will they not
be contented without difhonouring us by the peace ?
Believe me, the fcabbard is thrown away, if we cannot make the next peace as mafters, or as umpires
rather, we can only have the name of peace, with all
the expence, and all the anxiety, and more than all
the dangers of war. But if the war is to continue to
be carried on with the fame abfurdity and negligence, which has hitherto given us fo many occa-
fions for regret and confternation, there is no doubt
but that it will compel us to make fuch a peace : and
will not the King's fervants even *then* abandon the
ungrateful tafk to the friends of whoever may happen
to be the Briffot of the day; to thofe Britifh patriots,
the dearnefs of whofe connection with our enemies,

may

may win from their relenting nature, fome milder
terms of ruin, fome breathing time between the dif-
arming and the deftruction of Carthage?

The fituation of France is fuch, that fhe muft conquer and over-run all Europe, or be conquered and
reftrained by it. That nation, confifting of twenty-
four millions of inhabitants, is divided into foldiers
and hufbandmen ; and the firft clafs, let its loffes be
what they will, is perpetually renewed and recruited
from the fecond. Confifcation has hitherto reple-
nifhed the treafury : inftead of taxation, now an ob-
folete, or anti-revolutionary term, the pillage of the
rich, and the ranfom of the fufpected, have liberally
fupplied the enormous exigencies of the ftate. There
is no bankruptcy, becaufe there is no book : there is
no ftoppage, becaufe there is no account: without
foreign commerce, the affignat is neceffarily at par ;
and fince the danger is found fo great to poffefs, or
to be thought to poffefs, fpecie or bullion, it is not
impoffible that it fhould bear in its turn an agio over
thofe troublefome and perilous metals, againft which it
has fo long been indignantly difcounted : there is no
property but that of the nation ; every arm, and every
portefeuille, are at the immediate difpofal of the Convention ; the whole treafure and force of the empire
are moved and directed by a fingle committee, which
poffeffes more power, and not lefs forefight and activity than Louvois and the minifters of Lewis the
Fourteenth : and never did the vain device of that
ambitious

ambitious tyrant, in the zenith of his afcendency over Europe, become his efcutcheon half fo well as it would thefe new and fanguinary colours, which oppofed to all the earth, have fcarce loft an inch of ground in the extended ftruggle. To conceal the ftrength and refources of the enemy, is, in my mind, as weak and vain, as it is cowardly and bafe. What hope that we fhould refift and furmount the dangers which we tremble to look upon, and which thofe who lead us to the onfet conceal with fraud and artifice from our eyes? We are told, however, that fuch a fyftem cannot endure; that thefe violent exertions muft end quickly in laffitude and impotency. I am not of this opinion. I think this fyftem, and thefe exertions, may very probably outlaft every other fyftem, and conquer all other exertions: and I think fo, becaufe I obferve thefe other fyftems not only to be decayed and corrupted, but impelled and precipitated to their fall, by the folly or treachery of thofe who ought rather to repair and invigorate them, and becaufe I obferve thofe exertions directed rather to defend the rottennefs and vermin of thefe fyftems, than to oppofe the fhock from without, or to ftrenghten the arfenal within.

The enigma of the ftate of France is fimply this, why do men fubmit to be placed in a ftate of perpetual requifition; how have they been induced to believe that in whatever they acquire or poffefs, that in their houfes, their fields, and their bodies, they are only truftees and fiduciary committees for the public? Neither terror nor enthufiafm appear to me to account fatisfactorily for this moral phænomenon; individuals have felt, or profeffed to feel, this fublime of patriotifm, in every age, becaufe in every age, admiration and popularity have been difcounted againft tranquillity and againft gold : but fuch a fen-timent has not become common or univerfal, not-withftanding the fophiftry and the panegyrics of fo many orators and philofophers, and the romances of fo many poets, and hiftorians. In the Fable of Cur-tius or the hiftory of the Decii, there is here as much of vanity at leaft, and there as much of defpair, as there is of patriotifm and felf-devotednefs to the pub-lic caufe; the deed of Brutus, Manlius, Virginius, and fo many others, were no doubt held up rather as objects of admiration in the fchools of Rome, than of example and imitation; the fternnefs and ferocity of the Roman character during the republican age, have probably been chiffelled in a deep relief by the beft of their hiftorians, who when they fpoke of the an-cient manners and fimplicity, betrayed frequently as much as it was fafe for them to do of their antipathy to the corruption and abufes of their own age.

The drama of Corneille, and fome of the plays of Shakefpear have familiarized the moft enlight-ened countries of Europe with this caricature of their manners, and the effect of that vulgar and exaggerated opinion, has been frequently very di-ftinct in the progrefs of the revolution. We find the younger Brutus fpeaking with doubt and dif-

3   fidence,

fidence, and confoling himfelf at length by pro-
found reflexion, and philofophical arguments, for
that extraordinary act, which has made him fo celebrated amongft mankind. *Poftquam illud confcivi fa-
cinus*, is an expreffion made ufe of by himfelf with regard to it; and in the whole of the letter in which it
is to be found, if my memory does not deceive me,
you will obferve him fpeaking of it, not only with
modefty but with doubt, and anxious to juftify it to
hisown mind, rather than to vaunt or boaft of it to his
vain, but wavering correfpondent. But it would lead
very far from the object of this Letter, were I to undertake to defend the republicans of Rome from all
that imputation of ferocity, which, I think, has very
unjuftly been faftened upon their manners. It is fufficient for my argument that their *facinora*, which I
underftand rather in a doubtful than an accufatorial
fenfe, made very few profelytes amongft them, and
never converted any fect or fociety of men, much
lefs the majority or mafs of their nation; and I fhould
think it a fair inference, that the barbarities and maffacres of France were as little calculated to operate
fo general a converfion; as for terror, I think it
might have had its effect, while the nation looked
calmly down upon the crimes of its firft knots of ban-
ditti; that it might have impofed a momentary aftonifhment or filence, while the firft heads were fpiked,
and the firft victims mangled at Paris, but that it
never could have caufed all that activity, all that concurrence and competition in cruelty, that rival race

in

in guilt and horror that has been run by every department, every diftrict, every municipality, every contemptible club and fection of the empire. I think, therefore, we muft look for fome other principle to account for the extraordinary fpectacle which we are confidering. Thefe men who fuffer fo horrible a ty-ranny, who breathe fo oppreffive a fanaticifm, why do they fubmit to it? becaufe they eat, becaufe they drink, becaufe they have a phyfical fufficiency, which the hard heart and habitual tyranny of their Lords denied them before. The French, I believe, in my confcience, are the moft corrupt, the moft wicked, and the moft fanguinary nation upon the face of this earth, but they are not a ftupid nor a dull one. They compare the paft tyranny with the prefent, and prefer the prefent, becaufe the firft, like the interrogators of their Baftilles, reduced and exhaufted the body before it began to intimidate or excruciate the mind; and the fecond, with all its cruelties, at leaft accompanies the prefs with the bounty; and though it forces them to fight, both feeds and rewards them for fighting. The French people, therefore, are doubtlefs happier fince the Revolution than ever they were before it, for this plain reafon, that they eat and drink, and their health and fpirits encreafe with their republicanifm. They do not, indeed, perceive, that the banquet cannot laft at which all fit down; they do not read the writing on the wall, nor behold the ghoft of " Famine fcowling at the feaft ;" but " *plus fapit populus,*" fays Lactantius, I think, in his Trea-

tife

tife *De Divina Sapientia,* " *quia tantum quantum opus est sapit;* but whether he has said so, or I have dreamed it, I am equally convinced, that the French nation, in contradiction to the pusillanimous Manifesto of our own, is attached, and firmly attached by these powerful, these natural ties to the new form of its Government; and *this,* in spite of the new principles of *requisition and nationality,* which have hitherto defeated the calculations of Statesmen, and the confederations of Courts.

I shall now, Sir, if you will pardon me, for employing so much of your leisure, take some slight notice of the Jacobins, of whom I shall venture to speak in terms, rather unusual in this country, and very different from all that just horror, and that vulgar abuse which have been so industriously excited and directed against them. The Jacobins have committed no crimes that I know of, which have not been participated and avowed by the nation: even in all the series of emigrations, if I except the very first of all, and afterwards that of the priests, I can discover no emigrations but emigrations of Jacobins. The Feuillans, Monarchists, Constitutionalists, Ministerialists, Moderates, by whatever name they have been celebrated for a moment, what are they but Jacobins? Were the Jacobins less Jacobins when they were presided by Brissot than by Marat? Is Mirabeau less a Jacobin, that now his bones are turned out of the Pantheon? The fact is, every man while he moves on

with

with the ftream is Jacobin, and when he thinks of ftopping his career, or of breafting the flood, he becomes
Conftitutionalift, or fœderalift, or fomething elfe, no
matter what, the name of which is a paffport to the
guillotine. The Jacobins are neither more nor lefs
than the French nation, with the exception of fome
of the nobles and the majority of the priefts, and
though by their fuperior abilities and courage, fome
of them have been able to affume great power, and
to obtain a very high afcendency in the public councils, it is clear that they have accomplifhed thefe objects of their ambition, by complying with the unjuft
and interefted defires of the people, not by forcing or
tyrannizing their will, and that no crimes have been
committed that were not popular, and demanded by
the nation. Nothing can therefore be fo abfurd, fo
mean, fo pitiful, as to endeavour to reprefent them,
as a particular and infulated faction, who have ufurped the powers of government, and ftill retain them
in fpite of the wifhes of the nation, in favour of
Lewis the feventeenth; this miftake coft Monfieur
de Leffart his life, and five months imprifonment,
difgraced the Prince of Kaunitz, * for whofe dotage

* It is but juftice to the Prince of Kaunitz, to diftinguifh his
office from our own manifefto; his was abfurd, but it was not
indecent. In March 1792 the Conftitution prevailed, and the Jacobins or republicans were as much a faction as a great majority of
of any country is capable of being. In November 1793, the republicans were the conftituted authorities of the ftate, and the Britifh Miniftry renewed the abfurdity of M. de Kaunitz, with an impudence entirely its own.

it

it paffed, I believe very unjuftly, in the eyes of Europe, (for I can fcarce hefitate to think his famous difpatch was a mere *charte blanche*, filled up by the Auftrian Committee in the Thuilleries) and it is now again reproduced, with no better omens, in the manifefto of the Court of St. James's.

It is certain, however, that the Jacobins of to day, are of a deeper ftain than the Baillys and Fayettes who have faded off the canvafs of revolutions; even Briffot and Condorcet, that cold calculator of ufeful villainy, pretended to fome degree of humanity, when forced to oppofe the Marats and Dantons; and it is now very eafy to obferve the young ambition of Hebert and Chaumette, goading and pricking the jaded cruelty of the Robefpierres and Barréres; thefe men however will probably reign a little longer, and whenever they ceafe to reign, it will not be, becaufe their ufurpation is difcovered or their yoke uneafy, but becaufe they have not advanced in Jacobinifm as faft as the current of the nation, but fuffered themfelves to be furpaffed by men ftill bolder and more remorfelefs than themfelves. Were Briffot, or any of the twenty deputies who fuffered with him monarchifts? No: Was Charlotte Cordé a royalift? No: this affaffin was as Jacobin as Marat himfelf; fhe was a republican, and fhe was converted to the doctrine of the lawfulnefs of ufeful crimes. Clement, Ravaillac, would have been fuch republicans had they exifted in our age or had republicanifm been fubfti-

tuted

tuted to religion in their own. It is extraordinary that La Vendée with all its fuperftition, (for it is really fuperftitious and prieft-ridden) has not produced a fingle faint of this order, while infidelity feems to be fo fertile in enthufiafts and martyrs. Where are the figns of royalifm to be found in France? At Toulon? Surely not, for it is that very Conftitution they declared for, which has been found incapable of protecting royalty, and of which the republic is the true and lineal defcendant. But this they never dreamed of, till having failed in their plots of fœderalifm, and frightened by the punifhment of their accomplices at Marfeilles, and the flight of the Girondifts, they faw no hope of efcaping punifhment, but by calling in the combined fquadron, upon almoft any terms, to their protection. All the deputies expired invoking the duration of the republic.—But is it in La Vendée? Alas! It had taken refuge here with perfecuted faith; and here they both lie buried in one undiftinguifhed heap of cinders, a monument of the power and of the implacable ferocity of their perfecutors.

There is only one fenfe in which I can confent to confider the Jacobins as diftinct from the nation at at large, and that is as the leaders or Minifters of the nation; in that fenfe, I think, they would have the advantage in comparifon, over thofe minifterial factions which prevail in Courts, and adminifter fo frequently the affairs, in contradiction to the wifhes

of

of nations; and to confider them in this the worft point of view, I imagine they will not be found to be contemptible, fince they have hitherto fairly beat and outwitted every Court and Cabinet in Europe, in the ufe of fraud, bribery, and perfecution, thofe chief in-ftruments of our modern governments, and directed the force of their unhinged and disjointed ftate, with a degree of vigour, ability, and fuccefs, that ought to extort blufhes from other Minifters, who are at leaft as far removed from refembling them in their talents as in their crimes.—They are men, to ufe the words of one of our poets,

Fit to difturb the peace of all mankind,
And rule it when 'tis wildeft.

The Prince of Kaunitz-Ritzberg in March 1792, complained in the name of his fovereign, of the Ja-cobins, whom he called a *cabal*, and accufed of form-ing " *imperium in imperio*;" he even infinuated that while the Jacobins remained, the Emperor would not fee any fecurity in treating with the Conftitutional King. What was the confequence ? Did the majority of the people rife and fhake off the yoke of this pre-tended cabal, or did they adhere to the Jacobins to whom the imperial Philippic had lent frefh impor-tance and confideration ? The decree of accufation againft the Minifter followed inftantly, and the 20th of June, and the 10th of Auguft were but corollaries to the problem which had been folved with fo much

F   indifcretion.

indifcretion. How long will Minifters continue only
to imitate the faults and blunders of each other, determined to profit by no experience, and incapable
to act with common prudence and precaution?
When they declare from authority that the great majority of France is anti-republican, do they recollect
that what they announce with fo much triumph and
exultation at London, is either a lye or an accufation
at Paris? And that in either cafe it ftrengthens the
hands of thefe very Jacobins, who will convert it either into a caufe or pretext for frefh extortions, and
new requifitions, and make an engine of it to revive
the weary fanaticifm of the country, by frefh abjura-
tions and new invented oaths? Or do they calculate
merely for the meridian of London, and confider a
three-weeks delufion as victory and fuccefs, though
they expofe by it their own weaknefs, unpopularity,
and defpair to thefe very Jacobins, whom they would
be thought to deteft and defpife?

Now, Sir, fince I am engaged upon the fubject of
the Jacobins, and of the nation which they rule, and
having, I hope, declared my fentiments of the means
by which they rule, in terms which cannot be miftaken, though I fear they will not be imitated by his
Majefty's fervants, give me leave to fay thus much
of thofe deteftable principles, which it is thought
more loyal to abufe, than to forefee any danger
from the arms by which they are fupported, and
which it is become a kind of ton and fafhion to reject,

ject, not becaufe they are wicked or deftructive, but becaufe they are'ungenteel and uncourtly; I fay, give me leave to exprefs myfelf thus plainly with regard even to thefe principles, for even thefe ought not to banifh from our minds all remembrance of former oppref-fions, which have fo plentifully flowed from that great refervoir and fountain-head of human mifery, the Court. I think, Sir, and were I to be banifhed for faying it, I would confefs I thought it, that the crimes of France-free are too much detefted, if they make the crimes of France-enflaved, either regretted, or pardoned, or forgotten.

I know not whether the earth prefents not as fair a profpect to the cope of heaven, and to the eye of pure philofophy, overrun by the Tartar liberty that roves and ravages her untillaged bofom, as when de-jected, chained, and drowfy, fhe feems a frozen foot-ftool for the Sultan Power! A horde of tented Arabs on the free banks of the Tanais, is a nobler fpectacle of human fociety than a Conftantinople or a Vienna of cowled or turbaned flaves. The cataract that tears the rooted oak, or fweeps away the village, when its firft violence is fpent, defcends with gentler influ-ence, fupplies the rivulet, nurfes the vegetable herb, and grain, and vivifies the face of nature! But the ftagnant pool that fleeps and ftinks, where every rank weed *rots* and *rifes* to the furface, poifons the very air, excludes the beams of heaven, and makes no reparation to the polluted earth.—Courts, Courts!

Now,

Now, Sir, having faid fo much, as I have no doubt it will be reprefented, in *defence* of the crimes of the Jacobins, give me leave to fay fomething in extenuation, at leaft, of the conduct of his Majefty's Minifters; in truth I have fome doubt whether what I have to offer for them will entitle any hunter of comparifons to draw an analogy between thefe pages and the fabulous fpear, which healed, we are told, with one end as faft as it wounded with the other! But I have not much fear of being taken a fecond time for their partizan; and I owe it to juftice to fay what I know in their excufe. Minifters, I am aware, are too frequently but inftruments and utenfils in other hands. They obey too often where they appear to command, and follow only what others imagine and devife for them. The *Court*, the *Court*, the wealth, the patronage, the corruption of the Court, is the parent caufe of all our wrongs and all our forrows! Minifters are but the *inftrumenta Deûm*; though I will not take upon me to fay of what deities they are the inftruments, nor rake the peaceful rubbifh of mythology for the capricious or malicious gods that could employ or protect fuch inftruments. Could I but remove the veil that dims your mortal fight, as Venus did from her fon's, you would no longer rage and fret, and meditate revenge againft poor Helen; you would behold the golden trident that overturns our foundations; you would fhudder at the cruel Juno, that fits upon our gate, and calls in the hoft of crimes and vices that confume and deftroy our Ilium! While

this

this dreadful fource of every mifchief remains un
dammed, undrained, in the midft of us; while thefe
waters of bitternefs and corruption are permitted to
flow, with no dyke, no lock to reftrain them; while
by ten thoufand pipes and conduits they difperfe
their poifonous ftreams to every field and every little
garden, to every plant, and flower, and tree, from
the heel-root to the extremeft leaf, it will be vain to
look for wholefome fruit upon our blighted branches,
or noble timbers from our difeafed and enfeebled pith.

If Parliaments have ever been deceived, or corrupted,
or over-awed by Minifters, which I think no one can
be found to deny, have not Minifters been as frequently corrupted, and deceived, and intimidated by
Courts? But this Minifters will be careful how they
own, becaufe they feel more fhame in confeffing their
defpotifm than their fervility, and lefs fecurity in avow-
ing their weaknefs than their crimes. Are not Courts
then become too powerful for Minifters, as well as
too burthenfome for the people? And would not
Minifters gain as much in the independency and the
dignity of their fituation, by the reformation of
Courts, as the people would recover in the reduction
of taxes, and the return of morality!

There are two duties, of peculiar magnitude and
importance, incumbent upon Minifters at the actual
conjuncture of affairs; the one is to reform, and the
other to defend us. I will not debate their priority;
but what I will refolutely and eternally deny is their

incom-

incompatibility : The foreign war menaces every
rank and order of men, from the palace to the farm ;
and it does fo, not becaufe the greater part of France
is difpofed to declare for Lewis the XVIIth. but becaufe, excepting a few partial infurrections, not always in his favour, the totality of France is converted
to thofe theories of atheifm, " nationality," and
plunder, which it calls philofophy, patriotifm, and
equality ; not becaufe France defires the reftoration
of monarchy, but becaufe fhe is ready to emigrate
with her armies, and to over-run the earth with her
principles and her pikes ; not becaufe fhe is anti-
republican, but becaufe fhe is not only republican,
but, in fpite of the firft real conftitution fhe has ever
poffeffed, fhe remains revolutionary, and threatens
with revolution !—This is the reafon why, notwithftanding our apparent fuperiority, notwithftanding
our vain, but ineffectual parade of force, which we
difplay, like fome gorged or paralytic giant, without
fkill, activity, or prudence, and without, I fear, any
omen or favour from above; I fay this is the reafon
why we are in fo much danger from the foreign war ;
for I am not afraid to fay, that whoever pretends to
yield implicit credit to the Manifefto of the Minifter, " *dedit latus apertum,*" and cannot defend himfelf againft the arguments forpeace. Now, the reform, I mean if no innovation or fpeculation is
included in it, Sir, menaces nothing that I know of,
unlefs it be the Court ; and it promifes a thoufand
bleffings, not only to the farm but even to the cottage;

and

and accordingly we may obferve, without pretending
to any great degree of perfpicacity, how popular it is
in the country, how unpopular at St. James's!

We ought, no doubt, in candour, to allow for the
feelings of the Minifter, who muft have found himfelf
in an aukward and unpleafant predicament, becaufe
no man had contributed more to expofe and revile the
corruption of Parliament, nor animated in fo great a
degree the refentments of the people : The coarfe libels of Mr. Paine had difturbed the fleep of the ignorant, but the eloquent appeals of Mr. Pitt had convinced the wife, alarmed the timid, and determined the energetic and the free : He had raifed a
fpirit in the country, and the fpirit he had raifed had
ferved him with zeal and with affection ; it had la-
boured for his interefts, and ufed its innocent magic
in his fervice with fidelity and with fuccefs. It had
conjured him into power, and had rivetted him there
with an irrefiftible, but fecret fpell ; yet ftill, from
time to time, it put him in mind of the liberty he
had promifed, and demanded the performance, after
every labour, and at every turn ; but when he had
fatigued, and difpirited, and difappointed his little
Ariel fo often, that it moped and fulked, and hung
its wing, and difobeyed, or obeyed unwillingly, inftead of the free elements to which he had promifed
to reftore it, " he wedged the delicate fpirit in a
rifed oak," and betook himfelf to that foul witch,
who had fo long ufurped- the ifland ; he formed.

an

an accurfed confpiracy with that detefted *Sycorax*
the Court, and prepared himfelf to act

" *Her earthy and abhorred commands.*"

It will be curious, my dear Sir, to confider the
language the Court muft have held to the Minifter
upon this honourable and difinterefted occafion. Perhaps might it have faid, " You may become a little
unpopular, from undertaking my protection at this
time, and defending all my avarice and prodigality,
all my meannefs and oppreffion; but it is not my cuf-
tom to receive or offer friendfhip empty-handed; I
have fomething to confer, as well as to obtain : The
reform is my enemy, the war is your danger; now as
long as you will protect me from reform, I will grant
you a perfect liberty to conduct the war after your own
fafhion, with any degree of profufion, intrigue, negligence, or abfurdity, that you may judge expedient or
neceffary; my troops are ready, not only to defend
every crime or error you can poffibly commit, but to
perfecute whoever fhall dare to accufe you." Now,
Sir, would it not be lamentable, if fuch conditions
had been accepted, if fuch a treaty had been exe-
cuted, if a great and generous nation had been made
the victim, if liberty and virtue were the forfeit of a
Statefman's cowardice and a courtier's cupidity?
What think you would have been the anfwer of Clarendon, or his Southampton, to this vile and cour-
like propofition? I will not attempt to exprefs the
fcorn, nor paint the proud and virtuous indignation,

nor

nor that elated forehead with which they would have
rejected thefe " *dona nocentium*." " I will haften the
reform of abufes," would either of them have faid,
" not only becaufe it is honeft, but becaufe it is expedient : I will fatisfy the juft cries of the nation, not
only that it may be more happy, but that it may be
ftronger ; more able, as well as more willing, to fupport the burthens, and overcome the calamities of the
war : I will reduce the Court and the Civil-Lift,
which are unneceffary and inexcufable evils, that the
country may the better fuftain the war, which is an
evil inevitable and irremediable ; if there are grievances in the Government, if the Conftitution is impaired, I will redrefs thofe and reftore this, without
a moment's delay, that the people may have the full
benefit, and perceive the perfect excellence of that
fyftem, in the defence of which I am fo foon to call
for its treafure and its blood ; and that I may be
able to oppofe the enemies of that Government, and
of that Conftitution, with the united fentiment and the
united ftrength of the whole kingdom. And as for *you*,"
would he perhaps have continued, "for *you*, whofe vice
and avarice abforb thefe refources which might be carried to the war, who are the caufe of all the miferies
and all the murmurs of the people, who prefume to
offer impunity, inftead of deprecating your own punifhment, and to forgive uncertain to be pardoned,
know, I defire not the protection that you can grant!
—If I am miftaken, if I am unfortunate, I will retire,
becaufe it is my duty neither to perfevere in error

nor

nor in misfortune; but if I am guilty, from what penalty can you fhelter me? From the laws; by what
means? By intrigue and corruption :—But can you
hide me from myfelf; can you exclude the reproaches
of my own mind; can you fhut out confcience, the
judgment of the Public, the dread of that of pofterity? Alas, banifhment and death itfelf are but a
form of words, compared with the verdict of our
own minds, with the fentence of the greatjury of all
our race!"

Such, I think, would have been, Sir, at leaft not
very unlike to it, the language of the only Minifter
I know of, who never dwindled into a courtier,
whofe affinity to a King never corrupted his heart,
whom neither power nor adverfity elated or depreffed; equal and juft in every turn of fortune, and
great alike, whether perfecuted by an ungrateful
Prince and a deluded people, or moderating between
their lavifh zeal and his unprincipled ambition; in
every ftage and character of life a generous and exalted perfonage, whofe memory will be dear to Englifhmen, as long as they have hiftories to read, and
it fhall be permitted to read them.

Jamais l'air de la cour, & fon fouffle infecté
N'altéra de fon cœur l'auftére pureté.

Would Clarendon, do you think, Sir, inftead of
preparing to acquit himfelf of both thefe honourable
duties,

duties, have abandoned this as the price of that, and bought the defpicable privilege of performing one *ill*, by the facrifice or defertion of the other? Would he have allied himfelf to a bafe and rotten caufe, for the fake of being obliged to ufe lefs energy or wif- dom in a found and perfect one, or of being able to cover a blot in the game by diffembling the value of the ftake? Would Southampton have left that manly and tender panegyric upon his friend, which it is impoffible to read without emotions of tender- nefs, and fentiments of gratitude and veneration, if he had not thought him able to reject the overtures, and repulfe the impudence of courtiers, with all the dignity, and all the fcorn, with which he was ufed to refift the arts and importunities of other favourites, no doubt as virtuous, and as refpectable as thefe?

I think, Sir, I fhall not, after what has been faid, though to fpeak truth, I have not ventured to fay it with all the precifion and perfpicuity of which it is fufceptible, (but you will eafily fupply that defi- ciency, and pardon any other) I think that I fhall not, after what has been faid, even as it has been faid, in- cur much danger of being treated as paradoxical, if I fhould venture to affert that courts are not only grown too powerful for Minifters, but that none would gain more by their reduction than Minifters themfelves, provided they defigned to govern by juft, by honourable, or even by popular courfes.

You

You have been pleafed to exprefs your approbation of thofe parts of my former letters, which related to the duties and conduct of their chiefs, and the compofition and management of minorities: may they make the fame impreffion upon the public mind, and upon the mind of thofe who are more immediately interefted in judging thefe things right, and in acting according to a right judgment of them. They may prevent (I think it is yet time) many a violent convulfion, perhaps many a defperate wound to our happy and glorious Conftitution. Give me leave at prefent to prefent you with a few thoughts that have occurred to me upon the fituation, duty, and relative interefts of Minifters and Courts. They will not, I fear, be fo pleafing as the others; I cannot contemplate the fubject with equal delight: my own obfervation of them, and the difguft with which all hiftory and experience have infpired me towards them, have made the contemplation of them painful to my mind: and I can dwell no longer upon the fubject, than I think neceffary to the object of my letter, and neceffary or ufeful to be underftood clearly by the public.

We have fome few years back, you will remember, heard it canvaffed with great earneftnefs, and decided, I think, with more heat, exultation, and triumph, than with either candour, deliberation, or juftice, that *the Minifter* is the Minifter of the Crown. If ever you, Sir, fhould, fortunately for your country, attain

that

that dangerous eminence, I think I know you will feel yourself the Minifter of the People. You will never remain in power, if you cannot ufe it for the benefit of the people. You will advife the King, and you will execute the King's pleafure, and you will carry his councils into effect, as long as you think them ufeful and honourable for your country; and when you cannot ferve him upon thefe terms, you will know the poft of honour is a private ftation; you will retire into your individual capacity; and you will watch with unceafing vigilance, and oppofe, with all the force and energy of your character, the meafures of thofe who will take your place upon other terms, and condefcend to be the King's Mini-nifters, in contra-diftinction to being the Servants of the Public. Give me leave then to afk of you, whe-ther when you had accepted that important poft, to which the confidence, the efteem, and the refpect of the people is fo neceffary, and fo indifpenfible—un-lefs you could confent to a fervile and mechanical execution of the views and pleafure of the Court, whatever they might be, whether poffeffing, and defiring to poffefs, no power, nor permanence in power, but what this confidence would give you, and which muft neceffarily encreafe every day, and keep pace with the fervices you rendered your country, and the gratitude with which it would repay them; I fay, give me leave to afk you, whether you could entertain any defire that the people fhould continue aggrieved and oppreffed under the enormous load of

the

the Civil Lift, merely to fubfidize a horde of mercenaries, in the pay and intereft of the Court, not
yours; nay, on the contrary, always intriguing to
govern or to perplex you, and always ready to vote
and to act againft you, as foon as it is difcovered
you are more the people's friend, than the friend of
thofe who fuck the blood of the people? Now, Sir,
were it to appear ever fo problematical, or paradoxical, I confefs I could have no fcruple to affert, that
by the abolition of this ufelefs and deftructive band
of janiffaries, every Minifter, who was fit to be one,
who loved his country, who refpected parliaments,
who defired the profperity of the nation, or the duration and integrity of the conftitution, would find
himfelf more ftrongly, more firmly feated in power,
and more independant too of every other power: he
would find himfelf freed from a thoufand intrigues,
impertinences, and vexations; and above every
thing, from that habitual cabal, that familiar fraud,
falfehood and treachery, with which he is furrounded.

The party that belongs exclufively to the Crown, in
either Houfe of Parliament, is certainly not the party
of the Minifter, though, during the pleafure of the
Crown, he may prompt its pliant voice, and command its proftituted fuffrage! Let him hefitate or
refufe to comply with the maxims or the command
of the court, this party becomes inftantly hoftile and
menacing; it enables the Crown to dictate to the
Minifter, and intimidates a mean or an interefted
Minifter, (and we have now no Clarendons or South-
amptons)

amptons) from refifting the dictates of the Crown. If thefe mercenaries were therefore reduced or reformed, the ftanding forces of the Court would indeed be diminifhed; but the Minifter would gain in independence on the one hand, more than he could lofe from his precarious and verfatile majority on the other: he would, it is true, count fewer *mutes* in the Houfe, and mufter a fmaller number of what are called *dead votes*; he would be lefs able to carry by violence, unwife or unpopular meafures in Parliament; but neither would he be obliged, nor perfuaded, nor intimidated into propofing them; he would be more free himfelf, as well as the Houfe, and the Country; and the confidence of the Country, which he could not mifs, would confer more real power upon him, than he derived from all the fycophants of the Court, and all the corruption of the Houfe. The King too would be reduced to what he ought to be, the Chief Magiftrate, not the Chief Politician of the kingdom; he would be ftronger and firmer in that popularity, which he muft gain to govern either well or happily, than he could be in any hurtful privilege which might derive to him from the decay, abufe, and rottennefs of our Conftitution, of chufing Minifters, or of carrying meafures, with indifference, or in oppofition to the fentiments of his people.

Now, Sir, let me afk of you, fuppofing there were really to be formed in this country, a national party,

upon

upon national principles; and fuppofing you were
placed where you fo well deferve to be placed, and
where you will one day, I do notdoubt, be called by
the voice of all the wife, and all the virtuous of your
country; whether you could hefitate to difband thefe
odious troops, and to pour back into the lap of the
people, that part of the Civil Lift at leaft, which is
allotted to their pay? Could the Minifter regret, or
could the people regret the difperfion of thefe hire-
lings, who are the tyrants of Minifters, as well as the
enemies and the famifhers of the people? Could the
dignity of the Crown be diminifhed, or compromifed, by removing that profligate band, which
alone could bring it into danger or difcredit with
the people—with the people, not fufficiently able to
diftinguifh between the ufe and abufe of any inftitution, for example, between a Crown and a Court?
But if Crowns undergo any great degree of danger in
Europe from the convulfions of modern opinions,
and the influence of new principles and fyftems of
politics and philofophy, they have been brought
into all their perils, and expofed to whatever hazard
they appear to run, by Courts; becaufe Courts are
believed to be infeparable from Crowns, and corruption, prodigality, avarice, and venality, are known to
be infeparable from Courts. But were the filth fwept
out of Courts, and were Crowns lightened and relieved from that mafs of meannefs, of vice and im-
morality, which rots or ferments around them; were
the taxes levied upon the fweat of the people to
                                            nourifh

nourish, and to pamper these useless drones, or rather poisonous wasps, that rob and sting society, were these taxes remitted to it, were the odious and insupportable object removed, at least further out of sight, or even reduced to a small part of its present volume, not only would Governments be more secure, but Kings would have nothing to dread, either for themselves or their succession. It is their *Courts* which create the danger; it is Courts which are to be defended, and not Crowns; but, unfortunately, Courts have the means of abusing the weakness of Crowns; and if Crowns will enlist in the cause of Courts, there is no doubt they must abide by the fate of the garrison.

If Kings did but perceive how much their pomp and pageantry, their style and ceremony, in one word, their *Court*, has cost them in the genuine love, in the simplicity of their people's affection, how far aloof it keeps from them the wife, the modest, and the virtuous; how it alienates the just, the generous, and the free; what envy and contempt it breeds, what discontent and indignation it nourishes, they would discover one great source of the republican spirit, which seems to menace the thrones of Europe, and they would hasten instinctively, as it is pretended of that harmless animal which is hunted for its perfume, to separate themselves from that swollen and fœtid bladder, which supplies neither force, nor vigour, nor enjoyment, but retards and delays their

G   flight,

flight, and betrays them to the purfuer by the rank-
nefs, as much as it invites by the riches it con-
tains.

But there are fome gentlemen (difinterefted no
doubt) who are extremely apprehenfive left the dignity of the Crown fhould be impaired or diminifhed
by the fweeping of Courts; it feems to be their opinion, that if fome of the ceremonial offices were abo-
lifhed, if penfions were limited, and finecures deftroyed, the Sovereign would be abfolutely deferted
and negleded by the nobility and gentlemen, by the
learned and virtuous of England! Such an opinion
is at leaft a libel upon a loyal and noble nation, who
will crowd around their King to do him honour or
fervice, and cover the Throne with their generous
bodies, as often as it fhall be expofed to danger or
contempt, and after this mean and mercenary crew
fhall have fled and deferted, and ftopped its allegiance with the ftoppage of its pay! It is only, befides, in times of ignorance, and confequently of
fear, that ftate and ceremony can impofe to any
great political purpofe upon the people; knowledge,
happily for mankind, as it fpreads amongft men,
equalizes them by rapid, but imperceptible de-
grees; and fhew and form lofe much of their
charms and preftiges, in proportion as a real underftanding prevails amongft men; Courts, when viewed
from afar, may refemble thofe ftatues of Phidias,
which prefented to the diftant eye, we are told, the

gigantic

gigantic forms of Jove or Neptune, all fmooth and gloffy bright, fhining with polifhed ivory and gold; but if you approached, and examined them within, you beheld the cranks, and nails, and fcrews and cements, the mortar, and rubbifh, the πολλην αμορφιαν, of their conftruction. Now, unfortunately for Courts, all this αμορφια is glaring to the eye, and few ftand at fo great a diftance from the Coloffus, as to perceive the fymmetry of its form, and not to perceive the filth and uglinefs of its compofition. But let thofe who think fo meanly of monarchs, and of nations too, as to imagine, that the virtues of the firft could not obtain the refpect and affection of the latter, without the aid of falaries and bribes: who think the wealth of the Civil Lift is neceffary to fubfidize the venal loyalty of Britons, and would corrupt us into virtue and allegiance, let thefe doughty champions for Courts produce the Monarch of Europe who enjoys a ftate or fplendor, though purchafed with the fweat and tears of millions, fo calculated to dazzle the eye and win the hearts of their people, as the mild and faintly luftre that beams around the brows of Wafhington; the parental dignity, the *pia auctoritas*, that diftinguifh and defend the firft citizen of America!

Thofe too who would trace the kingly government to early or to divine origin, might do well to remember, that their favourite prototype is *a King without a Court*. Indeed, what a King fhould be, and what he might have been, in the infancy and innocence of

fociety,

fociety, before craft and artifice, the worft vices of
the heart, were taken to be the excellence and perfection of the underftanding,—a father in the bofom
of his family :—Where have they read of his Minifters and Chamberlains, of his Grooms of the Bedchamber, Gentlemen of the Bedchamber, Lords of
the Bedchamber ? Of his Pages, his Mafters of the
Ceremony, and that endlefs chain of pride, extrava-
gance, and folly, which is politically, morally, and
phyfically, a curfe upon the country ? Had Abraham,
had Abimelech, Stewards of the Houfehold, Mafters
of the Horfe ? Of the Hawks, of the Hounds ? What
were the finecures in an Arabian tent, or the contracts for a progrefs from Kadek to Gerar ? How
unfortunate that we have no memoirs of their great
officers of ftate ; probably they bore as perfect a re-
femblance to our own courtiers, as the beft of our
Kings has done to the worft of the patriarchs.

Every form of Government, whatever be its peculiar excellence, has alfo fome correfpondent defect,
fome propenfity and bias to its fall. The violence
and injuftice of popular judgments, are, I think, the
immediate caufe of the ruin of democracies. Excef-
five inequality of wealth, the accumulation of offices
and honours, and their becoming hereditary, are the
paths by which ariftocratical inftitutions arrive at the
tyranny of a few or of one. But Courts are the peculiar vice and cordial rottennefs of monarchies ;
they corrupt and are corrupted ; they are oppreffed,
and they opprefs ; their beft virtues are the virtues of
                                                    flaves ;

flaves; fervile duties, perfonal attentions, and fidelity; but their vices are the worft that flaves can
own; for befides lying, flattering, and cringing, to
whatever is above, they are neceffarily callous and
cruel to all that is beneath them. The jealoufy of
the eunuch is greater than the hufband's; the tyranny of courtiers more intenfe than that of the Sultan: They are enemies to liberty, becaufe they have
fold their own; and to virtue, becaufe it ceafes not
to upbraid them with the barter.

Courts too, befide their profligate character, fo
deftructive of the national morals, are politically mif-
chievous, and full of danger, fince they have af-
fumed and ufurped to be an intermediate body between the feveral branches of the public authority.
They are interpofed between Kings and their people;
they damp the affectionate loyalty of their approach,
and convert their honeft love into a diftant awe, a
forced and cold refpect; and, on the other hand, by
the forms, the delays, and the difficulty of his ac-
cefs, they obftruct and impair the parental feelings
of the Prince in their way to the people. They become the channel of every grace and favour; even
the godlike prerogative of mercy flows through polluted ftreams, and crimes unpunifhed, are the price
of the careffes of a proftitute, or the importunity
a liveried companion. But thofe perfons who ar
anxious for the dignity of the Crown, will tell
again, that thefe bands of courtiers are neceffary

its fupport. Can any man ferioufly think, Sir, that the loyalty and affection of the nation are encreafed by paffing through fuch channels as a Lord of the Bedchamber, or a Chamberlain of the Houfehold?

Purior in vicis aqua tendit rumpere plumbum,
Quam quæ per pronum trepidat cum murmure rivum.

Do the loyalty and affection of the people flow purer through thefe leaden conduits, that communicate its wifhes, or its complaints, to the dull and diftant ear of royalty; does the cuftomary transfer of a fubject's petition to the tender feelings, or confcientious policy, of a Lord Chamberlain, encreafe the gratitude or the attachment of the fuitor? Or do even the Lords with white ftaves tranfmit the gracious pleafure of the Prince with more amenity, or with encreafed benevolence to his dutiful fubjects, the co-eftates of the realm?

And of what fervice, let me afk you, could a Prince, and a Prince that fhould be a ftatefman, or a politician at leaft; of what fervice could he think it to himfelf, or to his fituation, to have the fenfe of every favour he beftows, the gratitude for every gift he difpenfes, diverted from his own perfon to an office or an individual?

O fortunatos Reges fua fi bona norint!

With

With the power they have to oblige, with the facility
they enjoy to engage affection; with the prerogative
they poffefs of granting honours, favours, pardons,
and exemptions, to be lefs beloved, lefs popular,
than their own fervants! Can the Prince be made to
believe, that it promotes his fervice, or attaches men
to his perfon or his caufe, that the chief of a party,
or his dependants, fhould nominate to offices, fhould
fill up vacancies, and that all the hope and all the
gratitude of the nation fhould be withdrawn from
himfelf, to crowd the train of fome Neckar or Seja-
nus?—Can he be ignorant of the cypher he becomes
at his own levee, where every vow is fecretly addreffed to his own fatrapes and officers, and himfelf remains at beft but the mandarin with the longeft
nails, too remote from affection, too ftately even to
be feared. Alas! why does it appear infeparable
from royalty, to feek to remove itfelf to an unmea-
furable diftance, to plant an hoftile and impaffable
barrier between itfelf and the people?—The people
who give it, fweat for it, bleed for it?

There is yet another point of view, in which it
may be expedient, at fome fitter opportunity, to confider the Court; namely, as the capital of the great
pillar of ariftocracy. At the prefent, I fhall content
myfelf with fubmitting to you, Sir, whether it were
not more wife, more natural, and more fortunate, if
the *politica! order of nobility* appeared to poffefs more
intrinfic dignity of its own, a higher fenfe of its ex-

alted

alted privilege and independent ftation, with fome-
what lefs of eagernefs and anxiety for the fmiles and
favours of St. James's ? Whether that body, which
is intended by the Conftitution to be a check and
controll upon the Crown, as well as the Houfe of
Commons, might not enjoy its great prerogative in
more fecurity, and acquit itfelf of its illuftrious duties with more effect and authority, if it were too
proud to divide the infamous bounty of the Court,
upon the one hand, and too honeft to feduce the
frail integrity of an indigent elector on the other?
If it fcorned to fhine with borrowed rays, and re-
volve in an orbit not its own, a cold and fervile
moon to a mightier planet, whofe courfe it ought to
regulate, and incline by its own volume and attrac-
tion?

" *Repetenda eft,*" fays Cicero, fpeaking of the
noble order of his own countrymen, " *repetenda eft
vetus illa feveritas, fiquidem auctoritas fenatûs, decus,
honeftatem, laudem defiderat, quibus hic ordo caruit ni-
mium diu.*" And it cannot have been faid with more
truth of the Roman, than it might be faid of the
Britifh Senate; for the corruption of both has derived from the fame fource; and the reigns, if I
may fo call them, of Sylla and Pompey, by fetting
up the protection and favour of a Court as an
object of ambition, and fometimes of fecurity,
had only done that, which has been accomplifhed,
in a greater degree, by the longer operation of the
fame

fame caufes in Britain. It had withdrawn the Senate
from the proud contemplation of its own independence and dignity, and delivered over the Senator
to fpeculations of individual greatnefs and advantage, from a corrupt compliance with the views, and
a corrupt hope from the gratitude of the Executive
Power.—In England, I am fure, one good confequence would have been felt at this time, if the
laws of our political fyftem had not been violated by
the magnetifm of which I have complained: The *Political Nobility* would not have been confufed and amal-
gamated with the *Court Nobility*; and the ariftocracy
of Parliament would not have been debafed and de-
preciated by that impure alloy of the ariftocracy of
the Palace ; the nobles of the nation would not have
been prefided by the *Liberti* and *Libertini*, the freed-
men and parvenûs of the houfehold : The names and
virtues that are dear to the country, the Ofbornes
and the Ruffels, the Bentincks and the Cavendifhes,
would not be eclipfed by the fudden elevation and
fplendour of fome ennobled (not emancipated) flave,
whofe enormous wealth, and refiftlefs favour feem
defigned for no other ufe nor objeƈt, but to fhew a
repining people the caprice of his fortune, and the
cruelty of its own !

While the Æmilii and Camilli were diftinguifhed
only by the dangerous popularity of a race dear to
the Romans : Pallas, Callifthus, Nymphidius, whofe
new honours had eternally difhonoured the fenate of

Rome,

Rome, and whofe names I blufh to remember, were tyrannizing and corrupting the empire.

Much, Sir, has been faid of late againft this order of the State, and it has never been fo well defended as it might have been; and this, I think, for want of making the diftinction I have juft pointed to you. *Nobility* is the blood of thofe who have faved or died for their country: there is an eternal ariftocracy in the gratitude of nations to the pofterity of patriots and heroes, and in thefe an eternal obligation to emulate the deeds and virtues which have endeared their names to their country. This is the true and folid bafe, the foundation and corner-ftone of genuine Nobility; and it will refift the wild and fenfelefs efforts of popular malice and captious philofophy: if it be not betrayed and undermined by the fpurious nobility of Courts; by the contempt and odium infeparable from a profligate or venal diftribution of honours. The prince who ennobled his proftitutes, and he who fhould openly beftow the peerage at the *recommendation* of his Finance-Minifter, infringed, or would infringe, the firft and fundamental privilege of that Houfe of Parliament, and give a deeper ftab to the political ariftocracy, than a thoufand Mirabeaus and Syezes could ever have inflicted.

One word more upon this important topic, which I find it difficult to relinquifh, and upon which I reprefs myfelf almoft in vain; we have feen with general

neral fatisfaction, even in thefe times, the high fpirit
of our real nobility difdain the charm of office, and
all the bribes of power, when this vulgar greatnefs
could be retained no longer without facrifices of honour : at the fame time that we beheld, with fenfations
which no language that I am mafter of can defcribe,
our artificial Lords, the *Court Nobility*, fucceed to the
vacancy, or remain in their offices, chaunting the
palinody of their own declarations, figning the retrac-
tations of their own counfels, without feeling humiliation, or confefling fhame.

But it were unreafonable, perhaps it is unjuft, to
expect fuch facrifices from fuch men ! Alas ! how
fhould they think of retirement ! Their woods are not
ready to conceal them ! It is furely but good-nature
to give time to the trees and the builders, before we
fend in the family ; and it would be cruel to divert
from their young plantations the ftreams that flow
four times a year; enriched with prolific flime from
the Treafury !

Serioufly, Sir, we ought not to exact efforts of virtue, or of courage, foreign to the principles and ha-
bits of men. To be happy in feclufion, we muft
bear along with us the regrets at leaft of others, and
our own applaufe. Retirement without repofe, and
folitude without a contented memory, are but vain
opiates, full of difturbed and reftlefs dreams, and do
but

but irritate the fever of the foul by forced and violent abftractions.

And when I fpeak of retirement, it is ncceffary to remember, that to the wife and virtuous, it brings fociety, domeftic joys, the offices of friendfhip, and the teftimonies of efteem, with all the *jucunda oblivia* of a bufy life ; but to difappointed vanity, and dif-carded meannefs, it prefents a defart, a wide and dreary void. The fhade is dark and gloomy which no reflection chears, no horizontal beam enlivens in the crimfon evening of life's *dufty* day. The palm obtained without a fingle public or private virtue, fheds neither peace nor honour over the purchafed palace. Forgive me, but when I think of the latter end of thefe dupes, I will not call them favourites of fortune, and of their vows conceded by malignant deities, I cannot refrain from reminding you of a wifer and a nobler prayer, and the wifh of one who had been truly great, if he had never been condemn-ed to be a Courtier.

Sic cum tranfierint mei
Nullo cum ftrepitu dies
Plebeius moriar fenex !
Illi mors gravis incubat
Qui notus nimis omnibus
Ignotus moritur fibi !

To thefe beautiful and well-known lines, permit me to add one brief reflection, which does not feem to

have

have occurred to Seneca, and which I fhould be forry fhould efcape your obfervation. There are men fo different from him, and they are not *plebeii fenes,* but have grown old and noble *cum ftrepitu* and *cum pulvere,* in dirt and noife, that folitude is therefore terrible to them, becaufe it will not permit them to die unknown to themfelves, but ftops them on the brink of death to form this late and painful acquaintance, and compels them to concur before they part in the fentiments of all their contemporaries !

It is not my intention to exhauft this endlefs fubject upon the prefent occafion; I have only fkimmed the furface with a light and rapid hand. It certainly feems to me important at the prefent conjuncture, to direct the public attention towards the Court, and to open the eyes of the public and of the Court itfelf, with refpect to their relative fituation and intereft; but it is enough to prefent the nuifance to the moral grand jury of the nation, and to deftroy the falfe opinion, that the Court is any part of the Conftitution of Great Britain; certainly it is neither a vital nor an integral part of it. It appears to me, I confefs, to grow a fungus out of the decay and rottennefs of other inftitutions, and to be a foul and ugly wen, or rather a rank and dangerous cancer upon the body politic. Let it look to itfelf! It is time when the eyes of the country are turned towards it. No man can deteft more than myfelf, as you well know, Sir, the operations of ftate-furgery; but it is proper that

this

this wen fhould learn, that if will not take phyfic, and reduce itfelf, the knife may be applied with perfect fecurity to the Conftitution.

I will now go one ftep further; and I will tell you (though thefe are times which require circumfpection, and we poor hares cannot make ourfelves quite fure that our ears may not be taken for horns) that the people defire, and muft have reform. The truths of Mr. Paine have been more confounded with his treafons, by the arts of interefted governments, and the chicanery of impudent lawyers, than his treafons have been with his truths, by the plain fenfe and fincerity of the people. The firft effect of his publications was alarming; the fuddennefs with which certain truths were let in upon the eye, both dazzled and confounded. The infidioufnefs with which abftract and impoffible perfection was held up to view, was itfelf dangerous, as light is to thofe who have long been immured in darknefs; and the hatred and contempt of all governments, fo induftrioufly infpired, and fo plaufibly defended by the eafy and fudden difplay of their enormous defects, abufes, and corruption, formed together a crifis, which providentially has not proved fatal to fociety. But it is not only Mr. Paine, and the abettors of fuch wild and fanciful doctrines, who have polluted and poifoned the public mind; other writings have been poured profufely into the world, and diftributed with equal induftry and perfeverance, in a caufe, I think, not

purer,

purer, nor more honeft than Mr. Paine's! The danger is not indeed equal, becaufe the fleep of defpo
tifm itfelf is preferable to the eternal convulfions of
an organized anarchy, and a fyftematic ftate of revolution; but I doubt whether it be a nobler principle
to corrupt into flavery, than to inflame to licentiouf-
nefs; whether it be bafer or wickeder to forge the
pikes, than the chains of the people!

When the Court and the Miniftry had made common caufe, and agreed to refift and to calumniate
every fpecies of reform, it was politic perhaps to raife
a cry, but I think it was unwife to declare a crufade
againft the reformers—The Court refufed reformation becaufe reformation was a Jacobin pretext, and
fuch was the folly, or the infincerity, or the unutter-
able abfurdity of fome of thofe who cried the loudeft
for reform, that they confeffed they confidered the
reform they demanded as a revolution in the government. *Inde mali labes*—From that time, the Court
had a pretence, a weak one no doubt, and no doubt
a wicked one, but where the ends were fo virtuous
and fo honourable, it would have been a paltry and
and fuperftitious fcruple, to have enquired into the
delicacy or the purenefs of the means; the Court had
pretext at leaft, of which it did not fail to avail itfelf,
to decry every fpecies of reform, and to confound
every defcription of thofe who demanded it; to confound them at firft with one another, and afterwards
in a body with the Jacobins of Paris, as if it were

4   one

one and the fame thing to defire greater virtue and
integrity in the reprefentative branch of our own
Conftitution, and to applaud the horrors that had
defolated France; as if it were equivalent to murder
and maffacre, to defire fome limits to corruption,
and were become treafon, or regicide itfelf, to pro-
nounce the name of liberty, or to look back with*
wiftfulnefs upon the brighteft and pureft annals of
our own hiftory! Oh memorable delufion! Oh in-
credible credulity! Oh matchlefs example of political craft and folly, of fraud and faction, of fuccefsful
impudence and ambition!

Mr. Paine, however, is an enemy to every fyftem
and to every Conftitution! *What then?* He has convinced men, who are aware of the treachery with
which he writes, that there is much to be reformed,
and fomething to be atoned for in our government;
He has convinced men that reformation will not. be
more fpontaneous from a Houfe of Commons fo conftituted as ours; and that the finecures diftributed
amongft the members of oppofition, from an obftacle
to the people's demands, as ftrong and infurmount-
able as if they were held by the partizans of the
government itfelf; he has fhewn that the fupport af-
forded to the exifting abufes by Lord Grenville a Minifter, and Lord Stormont a Peer in Oppofition, is
alike natural in both, fince both are placemen; and
that abufes muft neceffarily be perpetuated and encreafed under fuch a fyftem of corruption as this is,

which

which pervades every branch of the Government, and
of the Oppofition too : without purfuing the reafoning of Mr. Paine, which in whatever fpirit it is written, is fometimes folid and convincing, I fay convincing, for *fas eft et ab hofte doceri*—and is moft dangerous
perhaps where it is the falfeft and the moft metaphyfical; without purfuing Mr. Paine's reafoning any far
ther, and avoiding, as I do by defign, to enumerate
other inftances which occur to me of finecures held
by rich and noble families, on both fides of both
Houfes of Parliament, becaufe I think it unpleafant,
or perhaps invidious to point out gentlemen who have
fo much to anfwer for, without being in refponfible
fituations; I do not diffemble that it is my earneft
wifh, that there fhould be no fecret in the whole
kingdom with refpeft to thofe who are now fecretly
attached to the caufe of corruption and abufes, by the
falaries they draw from them. I think it hard at the
fame time upon Minifters themfelves, that Peers, at
leaft, will not defend their own privileges and exclufive greatnefs, without being hired to it like the
underlings of the prefs or the treafury; and I pity
the difficult and laborious fervices of Mr. Long
and Mr. Rofe, as much as I refpeft thofe talents
for perfuafion which cannot perfuade a Peer to
vote in his own caufe, without giving him the
bribe defigned for a commoner, and I think it cruel
too, that no caft nor individual will defend his
own prerogative and intereft, unlefs he be paid
for it;—but though I think all thefe things, my

H   dear

dear Sir, I fhall leave a lift and catalogue of finecures and abufes, to be furnifhed by thofe who lament them lefs, and can bring themfelves to contemplate our mifery and depravity with calmer nerves and a more philofophical temper, than it is my lot to poffefs. It fhall not however be wanting when occafion demands it; it will make a fupplement, and furnifh no uninterefting comment upon our *livre rouge*— Would the people of this enlightened country give credit to me were I to tell them, without demonftrative proofs, the enormous fums they annually pay, to buy themfelves enemies, to bribe traitors againft their own caufe, to bind down powerful families in eternal hoftility to their liberty, profperity, and peace?

I am now going to afk you a queftion, which I doubt not you have already anticipated, though I fufpect rather with apprehenfion than impatience. I am going to afk you, whether you can believe, for an inftant, that any fet of Minifters could deliberately continue and encreafe all thefe abufes and dangers, which are fo many infults befides, and a cruel mockery upon the underftanding and diftrefs of the country, unlefs they wifhed them to arrive at fome fatal crifis, or expected fome dangerous climacteric? Would any furgeon neglect or foment fo foul a wound, unlefs he defigned to bring the fore to a gangrene, and an amputation?

As

As to thofe who deny the neceffity of reform, and pretend to be perfectly fatisfyed with the exifting fituation of government and the Conftitution; I will juft afk them, why in that cafe they do not provide for the fecurity and permanence of a fyftem they think fo happy and fo perfect? I will afk them, whether they can think any eftablifhment fecure, againft which its enemies can bring fuch charges as have been brought by the enemies of our own? If corruption be neceffary, as they pretend it is, (and who will deny that it is the neceffary refource of Minifters who have neither wifdom, nor virtue, nor real honeft popularity?) Can it be neceffary too that it fhould ftink in every noftril, and glare in every eye? Would it not be prudent to heap the dunghill on the other fide of the hedge, where the fchool-boys could not find it out, and rake it to the annoyance and offence of every nerve in the neighbourhood? For my part, if I wifhed to continue this abominable and immoral fyftem of bribery and burgage-tenure, I fhould be as eager to disfranchife Old Sarum and half the towns of Wilts and Cornwall, as thofe perfons could be who wifhed honeftly for a real and radical reform—and I confefs ferioufly, that thinking as I do, I fhould be very forry to fee juft fo much done and no more; becaufe I am convinced that every abufe and injury that has not become plain and palpable to the people, may be continued, and will be continued, with unfeelingnefs and with impunity, as long as the wealth and fatellites of the Court, fhall be able to corrupt or intimi-

date

date every Adminiftration. It is here that every argument will return; it is here, that whoever would
fave his country from revolutions, the event of which
no man is able to forefee ; and whither men can be
driven only by the violence of their paffions, excited
more by contempt and infult, than by the fenfe of
habitual wrongs: It is here, I fay, that every friend
to England muft look for, and muft carry reform ;
without this, we can have no fecurity for the freedom or independence of any Parliament : we can feel
no hope of the integrity of any Minifter, of the duration of any fyftem, of the period of any evil.

The enormous power and preponderance of the
Crown, the excefs of falaries and penfions, the number of finecures, and places without number, have
united a formidable phalanx, more formidable from
the ground they occupy, than from their fkill, their
courage, or their refources: All thefe will affemble
to plant a barrier between the people and its wifhes :
But heaven forbid that an enlightened Prince fhould
range himfelf on the fide of a bafe and abandoned
Court, againft a patient, a loyal, and a virtuous
people! But heaven forbid, that a patriot King
fhould hefitate between a nation and the furniture of
a drawing-room, or know a doubt between the millions he was born to blefs, and the harpies who fteal
the viands from their lip ; who fteal the viands from
their lip, and poifon the fcraps they leave, with their
naufeous touch, and their corrupt effluvia.

The

The unexampled rigour of the courts of juſtice will, in my apprenſion, produce but a very momentary effect, and that effect will be followed by a direct contrary impreſſion. Far be it from me to enter into the defence of thoſe who have been condemned by a verdict of their country; however it may be to be lamented, that the ſentences pronounced upon them ſhould have appeared ſo generally ſevere, as to have diſmiſſed the audiences from our tribunals of juſtice with an enthuſiaſm very unlike to that which aſſembled them : In ſome places they ſeemed to feel themſelves not ſimple ſpectators of a trial, but entruſted with the character of the Chorus at leaſt in the antient drama; to have breathed their ardent vows to heaven.

Ut redeat miſeris abeat fortuna ſuperbis.

That they ſhould have ſeparated with ſentiments like theſe could have been more properly conſidered as unfortunate, if it ought not to have foreſeen and expected : the hardſhip of ſome trials, and the ſeverity of ſome ſentences, which I do not think it neceſſary to cite, have done more real miſchief to Adminiſtration than any libels, or any treaſons, which the objects of all this rigour were capable of writing or diſperſing among the people. Eager proſecutions and exceſſive puniſhments againſt this ſpecies of crime are amongſt the ſigns of the weakneſs, as well as the violence, of the fears, as well as the fury of Governments—the fever

H 3 that

that makes power mád, makes it tremble too; it
fhakes long with the fit, which made it ftrong and
terrible for a moment :—Fear is conftantly cruel, but
the fenfe of fecurity is naturally kind and forgiving.
Julius Cæfar could pardon the lampoons of Catullus,
but Afinius Pollio, or Caffius Chærea, I think it was
one of thefe perfonages, and I cannot go to book
for them, was forced to die for a compliment to the
memory of Brutus, and his brother-in law.

There feems, indeed, to enter as much fpleen and
bile into the conftitution of political as of natural
bodies. Republicanifm has frequently meant nothing but the hatred of monarchs : and 1 think that
I could fhew that in the ftates of Greece, and republican Rome, there prevailed more virulence and
malice againft kings, than love or underftanding of
liberty; this was, perhaps, the natural effeft of the
experience they had had of them ; for how many
have been fit to be entrufted with the conduft of their
fpecies ? Flattery can go no further than to compare
the beft of them living with one or two, and to diftinguifh and contraft them from all the reft of their
order—*Quomodo Auguftus fic et Antoninus*—and Hiftory, which judges all men, has her crofs to make
againft the very prototypes of perfeftion *. The
great political fecret was not yet difcovered, that

* *Non fu fi fanto ni benigno Augufto,*
  Come la tromba di Virgilio fuona.

Kings

Kings might be tolerated even in republics, and
Freedom, a Chareatid nymph, fubmit her generous
neck to the gentle burthen of a legal and limited
throne : Androcles had not tamed his lion ; and Liberty, leading a muzzled monarch by her fide, had
been a bolder hieroglyphic than Œdipus and the
Sphynx herfelf would have dared to decypher. Even
now, how few ftates of Europe, adminiftered under
republican forms, have any juft idea of liberty ! In
Venice, where there is a direct, intenfe, and meridian
political tyranny, the people exult, becaufe they have
no King; even in Holland, what notion do they entertain of reprefentation ?

We read but of one people, however, who have
rejected liberty; the Cappadocians, we are told by
Strabo, as he is cited by Lord Bolingbroke, *Liber-*
tatem, repudiaverunt ut quam fibi dicerent intolerabilem ;
I fufpect, however, that this determination of the Cap-
podocians, in effect, was little more than a compliment to Rome, and regarded no part of their own political conftitution, fo much as the refidence or ab-
fence of a legate or his affeffor, (who might probably
have poffeffed fufficient intereft to procure fo loyal an
addrefs) ; but of this I am confident, that freedom is
intolerable to every vicious and corrupted people,
whether they have the means of rejecting it or not,
as we may contemplate it in France, where it is new ;
and, I am confident, that it will be moft intolerable to
a corrupted people, where fhe has long been eftab-

H 4   lifhed,

lifhed, as I hope we fhall never be able to learn by an example ftill nearer home; for though in a depraved ftate, in which liberty is new, fhe may be violated and abufed, fhe can fcarce be made the bawd and pimp of defpotifm, or turned into a ftate-engine and pretext for oppreffion : but in a country which has long been free, but has ceafed to be fo, becaufe of its corruption, fhe will eafily become all thefe, and worfe, if there is worfe than thefe; the names, the forms, and even the memory of the antient freedom, will become not only decoys and fnares, but crimes and treafons, wherever they are difcovered; it is there that fighs will be regiftered, and regrets indicted, that thought will be dogged by danger, and filence haunted by fufpicion : In fuch a ftate, the laws will not be abrogated nor forgotten, but they will be ftrained and perverted ; a fpecies of horrid mockery will be engrafted upon oppreffion, and the virgin be delivered to the hangman's luft, that fhe may pafs *legally* to the torture or the fcaffold.

In mixed Governments like our own, it is natural, perhaps it is unavoidable, that fome of the citizens fhould incline with predilection and favour towards one branch of the Conftitution, and regard the others with jealoufy at the leaft : Amongft the fubjects of fuch a ftate, there will be fome who may miftake themfelves into an exclufive loyalty and attachment to the regal branch, incompatible with the prin-ciples of free Governments, or the fentiments of free

Men;

Men ; while there will be others, whom an unmea-
fured love of liberty, and of the very forms of liberty,
may induce to lament the loft republic, and to offer
vows not very favourable to the monarchical part of
the Government ; there may be perfons too, amongft
either or both of thefe defcriptions, who may be but
ill affected towards the ariftocratic order, and averfe
to titles of nobility and hereditary diftinctions, which
have not, they may imagine, fo much decorated and
exalted the individuals who bear them, as they have debafed and degraded the great mafs of mankind, from
which they have invidioufly feparated and divided
them ; but none of thofe individuals, it is clear, can
be perfectly contented with the abftract theory of our
exifting Conftitution ; one will wifh that in the diftribution of powers, more weight had been thrown into
this fcale, while another will defire to give a preponderance to the oppofite fide of the balance : but bring thefe
men together, and they inftantly become contented,
becaufe they inftantly perceive the neceffity of mutual
conceffion and adjuftment. Three citizens, fuch as
I have defcribed, deputed to felect a Conftitution,
muft of neceffity form one analogous to our own :
virtus eft medium vitiorum & utrinque reducta. Would
it not therefore be tyrannical, unjuft, and abfurd, to
punifh any one of them for the eccentricity of his
opinion, fince the union of thefe opinions makes the
very fyftem which they all feverally prefer to the fyftem of each other, and which they all have made

their

equal facrifices to obtain? Were the Tories perfectly
fatisfied at the Revolution, did the Whigs carry all
their points? Was it not accomplifhed by reciprocal
conceffions, by mutual forbearance, by a compro
mife of political tenets and pretenfions? Is it con-
tended, that every individual of the ftate muft be
a bad fubject, who conceives a greater degree of perfection to be poffible in the Government, than he
perceives actually to exift there, or a jufter balance
and diftribution of powers than he believes is to
be found in our Conftitution? Alas, we are all
guilty, Whigs and Tories, Court and country, every
defcription and party of us are criminal before fo fe-
vere a tribunal!

Give me leave to take this opportunity of expref-
fing the regrets I feel, that the privilege of thought
fhould be allowed of to a greater extent in our fchools
and univerfities than in the great forum and theatre
of life. If we are to go on according to the maxims
now adopted, and become popular in Courts and in
Courts of Juftice, I am fearful we are guilty of a fatal
error, in teaching our children the republican lan-
guages of Italy and Greece, and in imbuing their
minds with principles fo likely to lead them to high
treafon as thofe of Tacitus, of Salluft, and Cicero,
of Plutarch, Xenophon, and Socrates. I think it is
Diogenes Laertius in his life of Antifthenes the philo-
fopher, who has the following remarkable fentence,

Te

Τον Σοφον ε καλα τας κειμενας Νομας πολιτευσθαι, αλλα καλα τον της
Αξελης, και ιξασθησισθα; δε : μονον γαξ ειδειαι τον Σοφον τινων χρη εραι.

I shall certainly not put this maxim into English,
because I cannot approve of all the discretion and
arbitrement it establishes in the breasts of learned
men; it authorizes them, no doubt to exercise their
judgment, at least upon exifting laws and conftitu-
tions, and more than to publish their opinions; but
still less can I applaud the axiom, that seems to prevail at present, and to make it treason or dishonour
to suspect, that there might be compounded a better
system of government, or invented a wiser code of
laws than that by which we are guided; though I
am firmly convinced, that all who aim at this greater
perfection, by any other means than by restoring
them to the purity they once enjoyed, and bringing
them back to the simplicity and virtue of their origi-
nal institution, will find themselves miserably mis-
taken in the experiment. However, while this species of persecution prevails, and even when it shall
have ceased, it might certainly be prudent to esta-
blish a greater degree of conformity between our laws
and our education; for surely, my dear Sir, it is
seriously to be apprehended, that it is not for the
happiness of the rising generation to be educated for
freedom and virtue, nor to become enamoured and
familiar with the great examples of free and virtuous
antiquity, at this period, when not only *corrumpere*
& corrumpi is the fashion of the age, but when there
is so much danger and disgrace in refifting the tor-
rents of fashion and corruption. Surely we do not
only

only nurfe their opening minds, " *nihil fanantibus lit-teris,*" but with dangerous longings, and with fatal affections ; we do not form them to be happy or contented citizens in fuch a ftate as ours, but bring them up rather to the pillory, to banifhment and the fcaffold ;—will they not one day exclaim againft us, nay, may we not ourfelves already cry out againft our predeceffors, as Sir John Savile did, " Oh, improvident anceftors ! Oh, unwife forefathers !" or may not even thefe fighs and regrets very foon become treafonable or feditious ?

With regard, however, to the terrors infpired, or capable of being infpired, into a whole people, it is worthy of remark, that men are more eafily afto-nifhed than they are frightened : though aftonifhment, particularly in political cafes, is frequently miftaken for fear. But there is this important diftinction between them, that though the impreffion is inftantaneous in both, its duration is different and un-equal.....Aftonifhment is rarely, or perhaps never followed by fear; for the very fenfe of recovery from it is active and encouraging ; men relieved from the weight of it, naturally turn to examine the object or the circumftance that caufed it, and courage always arifes from the minute examination even of real danger. But that torpor which you have obferved in the people, has its fource, according to my judgment, and according to my fears, in another, and a fatal caufe, in its contempt and equal indifference towards both Minifters and Oppofition ;

in

in its defpair of deriving any redrefs or remedy from either, and in the cool determination it feems to poffefs, to do itfelf that right which it thinks is impudently and unfeelingly denied to it on the one hand, and feebly and hypocritically demanded for it on the other. But if it does fleep, I would advife his Majefty's Servants to watch carefully and conftantly over its flumbers; its waking will be terrible, whenever it happens; and any clafh, in any part of Europe, may echo fo ftrongly in its ears, as to occafion it to ftart up unexpected and fudden. They who are fo well accuftomed to rock the baby, fhould be ready to hufh its cries when it wakes.

You know, my dear Sir, the apprehenfions I have long entertained of this *waking*;—what I have already written will always be a proof of the anxiety I have entertained left this Reform fhould be accomplifhed by other hands than thofe of Parliament: a Reform in any other way appears to me to differ in nothing from a Revolution: for if the power of the State exifts for a moment in any other body than in the Houfes of Parliament confenting with the Crown; it may exift there for a month, a year, for a century, or for ever. Firmly convinced in my own mind of the danger of this important crifis, to which we are made forcibly to approach by the ignorance, the obftinacy, or the defign of his Majefty's Servants; by the corruption of the Court, and by the perverfenefs of a majority in the Houfe of Commons: and ftill more

immediately

immediately by the abfurd and criminal ill conduct
of the war, which difgufts the people, more ftrongly,
and more fenfibly, than remote and habitual evils;
and teaches them to defpife Minifters, as well as to
hate them, (the moft dangerous of all fituations). Convinced of this danger, and alarmed at the difficulty
which every honeft mind muft experience, in chufing the part he will act, and even the fide upon which
he will range himfelf, I have felt it my duty, as a
good citizen (I pretend to no other title) to make
thofe fenfible of the peril who are able to avert the
ftorm, or affect to be able to govern the helm. And
furely if we can efcape the danger by throwing over-
board fome of that ufelefs lumber, and of thofe cumbrous impediments which I have already pointed out,
I think neither yourfelf, nor any good Englifhman,
will regret them: we fhall fail the lighter, the happier, and the fafer without them; more united
amongft ourfelves, more formidable to the pirates
and privateers, that envy our flag, or covet our car-
goes; and we fhall fail too, with better omens, and a
more favourable heaven!

As you are decidedly of opinion that the fafeft
and propereft method to obtain this Reform for
the people, in a legal and conftitutional manner, is
to develope the plan gradually and according to the
circumftances of the time; and as you are convinced
that it might now be granted them, with perfect
fafety, in a parliamentary manner, and by means fa-

miliar

[111]

miliar to our Conftitution; by fuch, for inftance, as
I have incidentally and occafionally pointed out in
the fecond of my letters, there will remain nothing
for me of much importance to fay upon that head,
farther than that the time ought not wantonly to be
fported with, nor any occafion fuffered to go by, of
giving the people an affurance at leaft, that it *can* be
done for them in Parliament, of which many of them
have began to doubt or to defpair; and to which many,
from frequent difappointment, as well I fear as from
other promifes and expectations, have grown very
indifferent.

I fhall now, before I take my leave of you, my
dear Sir, in compliance with your wifhes, which will
always be laws to me, but with great hefitation and
deference, fubmit to you a few thoughts upon what
might have been, in my humble opinion, the conduct of this war, and upon the expediency or propriety of making peace, which you feem to imagine
exifts at the actual conjuncture of affairs. Refpecting the war, I confefs, that as (owing to her infular
fituation, and the immenfe fuperiority of her maritime force, as well as the happy influence of her Conftitution, and a jufter diftribution of property, than I
think prevails in any other kingdom of Europe) the
danger could not be nearer, nor fo near to England
as it was to the ftates on the continent, it has appeared to me to be abfurd to thruft ourfelves fo for-
ward upon the fcene, and to affume the principal

2 character

character on the drama. It has always been the folly and the vain-glory of this country, to do every thing, and to pay every thing for all her allies; and God knows how long, how often, and how lately, she has had occafion to repent of the power her prodigality procured her of dictating in councils, where she difplayed none of the national qualities, excepting its vanity!—yet there were councils in which it would have been for her intereft, and for her honour, to have borne fway, where her afcendency would have been a common advantage to the caufe of the allies, and of humanity; and where, if fhe had bought or won the power to dictate, the benefit would have been acknowledged by Europe, and by mankind.

The war, Sir, was inevitable from the very beginning of the French revolution, notwithftanding the opinion of the learned gentleman who derives it from an act of their third Legiflature; and notwithftanding the manifefto of the Minifters, who feem to think that things cannot be placed upon a better footing than they were upon the 9th of Auguft, 1792.—But *Pace virorum tantorum*, the war was unavoidable from the very beginning and principle of the revolution in France: and it was evident that it was fo, to every man acquainted with the temper of parties, and the moral and political fituation of that kingdom. On the 10th of Auguft, however, by the confeffion of the manifefto, it became fo, and in truth, I know of no alternative of events which could have difpenfed with it, though there exifted, no doubt, the means of ac-

celerating

celerating, and of retarding it. Government diſſembled this neceſſity as long as it was able, and ſuffered
itſelf to be inſulted and injured, and puſhed to ex-
tremities, before it pulled of the maſk. Whatever
objections the other Courts of Europe, and the wiſeſt
of the Royaliſts, have made to this policy, I ſhall not
venture to blame it, conſidering the internal ſtate of
the country, which was neither ſerene nor ſecure.
This interval, Sir, however, I mean the interval between the depoſition of the King, and the declaration
of the war, ought, I think, to have been employed
by England in bringing the other powers of the intended confederation to a plain and unequivocal declaration of their ultimate views and intentions, and
in binding them by formal and explicit engagements,
both to the ſpecific conditions, and to the public object
of the alliance. Perhaps, Sir, for example, it would
ot have been unwiſe or improper to have ſtipulated,
that none of the high-contracting-parties, who were
to form this political cruſade againſt the crimes and
uſurpations of France, ſhould, during the actual
term of the contract at leaſt, *invade*, or *plunder*, or *divide*, the poſſeſſions and territories of any other ſtate:
That none of the powers who acceded to this engagement, ſhould adopt the principles of the Jacobins, againſt whom it was directed, or commit any
crimes which might extinguiſh or extenuate, by com-
pariſon, the horrors excited by thoſe which were
daily perpetrating at Paris; that it ſhould be held to
be as unjuſt and unlawful to hold a ſovereign pri-

I   ſoner

foner upon the banks of the Niemen as upon thofe of the Seine; by foreign, as by domeftic oppreffion; and be reputed as violent and arbitrary, to tear a province from a Republic as from the Pope himfelf.

When thefe preliminaries had been figned and exchanged, perhaps it would not have been found more difficult to have procured from the King of Pruffia in particular, our old friend and ally, diftinct and pofitive engagements, which might have prevented any treachery or interruption being given to the progrefs of the war, than it has been found to repair thefe *accidents of the alliance* by the remonftrances of my Lord Yarmouth or by the dexterity and addrefs of my Lord Malmfbury. This precaution, Sir, would, befides the important advantages it would have fecured to the Allies; befides the gates of Landau, which it would have opened; befides the influence it might have had in the councils of the Duke of Brunfwick, when the retreat from the plains of Chalons was under deliberation; I fay, befides this common beneñt, it would have faved much anxiety, much difhonour, and much expence to Great Britain. And though, indeed, the Earl of Yarmouth might not have been fo foon convinced, or fo eafily converted by the fyrens of the Rhine, yet the Goddefs of Perfuafion herfelf fate upon the banks of the Tagus, and beckoned him to the gardens of Aranjuez.

Serioufly,

Seriouſly, my dear Sir, it, appears to me to be worthy of all our regrets, for it is not our loſs, but our diſhonour alſo, that the interval of time which elapſed from that period when Miniſters were convinced, or ought to have been convinced, of the inevitability of the war, to the moment when the headlong violence and infatuation of France compelled the actual commencement of hoſtilities; that this interval ſhould not have been employed with more wiſdom, precaution, and political ſkill. The King of Pruſſia at leaſt, might have been induced, I ſhould imagine, to covenant not to diſturb, if joined to the Houſe of Auſtria, he had not been able to guarantee the tranquillity of Poland. But it occurred, no doubt, to our ſagacious and liberal Adminiſtration, that it was eaſier and more conſiſtent to ſecure Pruſſia by the abandonment of Poland, by a ſtrict analogy to that honourable principle which had induced it to ſecure the Court by the ſacrifice of the reform! And after all, are they to blame, if there are Kings more Jacobin than the Jacobins of Paris, and Courts more treacherous than the ſchools of Danton and Barrere?

I think, Sir, however, that the people of this country would have been better ſatisfied, if they had ſeen the extraordinary ability and peculiar talents of my Lord Malmſbury directed, during that interval, to the attainment of this object; and that at the preſent moment they would be happier to think them exerted to obtain, I will not ſay ſome aſſiſtance, but fome definitive explanation from that ambitious princefs, who feeds the flames and fury of contention with her refcripts and her manifeftos; who halloos on the dogs of war; but neither rifks her blood, nor exhaufts her treafure, nor fatigues her ftrength, by partaking in the chace: Of that ambitious princefs, who beholds with equal joy, difeafe, defeat, or fiege or famine, or maffacres or battles, thin the contending nations; who exults in the common ruin and defolation, and prepares herfelf to be the laft moft dreadful fcourge of our European world; fubduing us by wounds our own hands have made; founding her barbarous throne upon the ruins we have pulled upon our own heads; and enflaving us by our own madnefs, folly, depravity and crimes!

But if any meafures of prudence or precaution feemed beneath the grandeur and magnanimity of the cabinet of St. James's; or if the King's Minifters in fact knew nothing of the war till it was declared by the Convention, and Breda was invefted; if we are to date all their preparations from the embarkation of the guards at Greenwich, and the manifefto of General Dumourier: then, Sir, I cannot but acknowledge that their refentment was equal to their aftonifhment, and that they refolved to make the war every where with the fame wifdom that had made them expect it no where; and they divided their force accordingly into fo many different objects and directions, that in return they might furprize France every where, and be able to

make

make an impreffion upon her no where!—After the expulfion of the French from Holland, I believe I may fay the whole kingdom (I beg pardon of the Court, but I had really forgot it) was appalled and afflicted at the minifterial perfeverance in fending troops to Flanders; but I have already expreffed myfelf upon this fubject, and I had long before imperfectly conveyed my fentiments to the public upon the propriety of that meafure *. Some other material points in the conduct of this difaftrous campaign, I have examined in the early part of this Letter; it remains for me to fay a few words upon others, of which I have purpofely referved the confideration for the prefent opportunity, that their impreffion might not be diminifhed by the horror I am fure you have felt at the too faithful detail I have given you, of the corrupt and guilty caufes of fo many and fuch fatal confequences!

Of thofe vain and dilatory expeditions to the Weft Indies, after the unhappy attempts of Admiral Gardner, perpetually poftponed and facrificed by the folly and trepidation of Government, to new and fugitive objects, to wild and impracticable projects, to Dunkirk, to Toulon, to St. Maloes, but always to the favourite fcheme of Continental warfare and invafions; I fhall not permit myfelf to examine the details. The evident abfurdity and deplorable iffue of the at-

---

Vide Poftcript to the Firft Letter to Mr. Fox.

tempt

tempt againſt Corſica, has almoſt been overlooked
and forgotten in the general maſs of our errors and
miſcarriages, in the great total of public misfortune
and diſgrace! the imperfect accounts hitherto received from Toulon, make me neceſſarily reſerved,
though I cannot ſupprefs the whole of my ſorrow and
conſternation, nor conceal the diſguſt and ſhame
with which I have beheld that unhappy and diſho-
norable ſcene, which has cloſed our tragic pantomime
in the Mediterranean —I leave to others to lament
with real or affected grief, the miſeries of that unhappy city, and to deplore with feeling or eloquence,
the fierce revenges which deſolate her habitations. To
others I abandon the ſad and painful taſk of recapitulating our own loſſes, and of mourning the brave
and Britiſh blood which has ſtreamed ſo plentifully,
which has been ſo uſeleſsly, and ſo prodigally ſquander-
ed under its walls. To others I depute the invidious
labour of counting the treaſures which have been la-
viſhed to retain it, the penſions, ſalaries, and annui-
ties which ſurvive its ſurrender! I will confine myſelf
to one plain and diſpaſſionate argument, and I will
leave it to make its own impreſſion upon the unbiaſſ-
ed reaſon of the public, without any aid from an
arrangment of words, from reflexions of ſorrow, of
humanity, or if I can ſupprefs them, of indignation.

Either Toulon was tenable, or it was not tenable :
in the firſt caſe, it is plain, that it ought to have
been defended on the 19th of December; in the ſecond

cond, it ought to have been relinquifhed long before
the republican army was in fufficient force to compel
and to impede our embarkation ;—not a fhip, not a
military magazine, not thirty pieces of cannon, not
a quintal of gunpowder ; and much more, not a
man, or a woman, or a child, defirous to embark,
ought to have been left, or needed to have been left
at Toulon. No blood, no treafure, needed to have
been lavifhed there ; Sir Gilbert Elliot, and all his
fuite, needed not to have been appointed, nor the
troops of Naples, and fo many other nations, to have
been tranfported there. So many brave but unprofitable fallies, needed not to have been attempted ;
General O'Hara need not now be a prifoner, nor our
bofoms to be troubled for the fate of this gallant, but
unhappy Commander. There is blame fomewhere,
and it cannot be denied. Meffrs. Rofe and Burgefs, I
appeal to you once more ! Was it tenable, or was it
not fo ?—My opinion is that it was *not*, for I know
the valour and the fkill of the noble Lord who com-
manded the fleet, and of the General and troops who
were in poffeffion of the fortrefs ; and I think too that
it was. *not*, becaufe I know that the corruption of
the Adminiftration is as great as its ignorance, and
its profufion equal to every thing but its contempt
both for the public intereft and the public opinion.—
While Toulon ferved as a pretext for patronage,
while it furnifhed appointments and falaries, and
procured mercenary friends to the Minifter, Toulon
was *tenable* ; while it provided for their profelytes,

I 4

purchafed impunity for themfelves, Toulon was *te-nable*; while it conferred finecures and paid votes in the Houfe of Commons, Toulon was *tenable.*— But when the fyftem was complete, when the objects were attained, when avarice was gorged, and corruption faturated; when the ftipulated reverfions and the promifed penfions were merited and legalized, Toulon became *untenable*, though it was too ufeful to be abandoned till the precife moment of attack; the Minifters regarded it with affectionate regret, and, longed and lingered, till a great part of our moft important acquifition was neceffarily loft, till our blood had ftreamed, and the fhips and ftores which might have been brought off before with perfect fafety, were, I fear, but imperfectly deftroyed.

I will not give way to my feelings upon this fubject; but I fhould neither do juftice to the Public nor to myfelf, who have been once accufed of partiality to Minifters, if I did not declare, in the moft unequivocal and explicit terms, that here again is matter of IMPEACHMENT; that the marks and footfteps of corruption are plain and vifible through all this opprobrious tranfaction, and that it is the duty of every man, whofe talents, whofe zeal, or whofe induftry can enable him to fupply, in any degree, the irreparable deficiency of a virtuous minority in Parliament, to trace it to its laire, to that impure and naufeous den, where the monfter retires to devour and divide its prey........Oh, Sir, what might not, at this

this time, a virtuous minority, a national party, what might it not atchieve for the country? what might it not procure, what might it not prevent, what bleſſings might it not confer, what miſeries might it not avert from our heads and thoſe of our children! Yes, Sir, I have already ſaid it, but I muſt repeat it again and again, majorities may plunge us into diſtreſs, but minorities only can plunge us into deſpair—where are we to look for redreſs, and where for atonement? Who ſhall break that horrid contract, who ſhall finiſh the impunity, which is the ſource of miniſterial crimes, and the price of the public miſery and misfortune? Where are the defenders of liberty, where are the champions of the Conſtitution? Alas, our eyes ſeek them in vain, or weep to find them wandering, like ſullen ghoſts, in the aiſles and avenues of the Court, or hiding themſelves in the guilty crowd that ſurrounds them, from our reproving ſearch, from their own ſurviving ſentiments of honour—The ſuppreſſed, but inextinguiſhable flame of public virtue, ſcorches and conſumes the ſouls that have dared to deſert or to betray her!

Give me leave now to enter into a very brief conſideration of the proſpects of peace, and the opinion I am ſorry to ſuſpect you entertain of the expediency of the negociation!

The

The only found argument, I confefs, I have heard
for making peace, is the extreme imbecility and incapacity of his Majefty's fervants to make war, and
the danger of confiding the management of it to any
party that could fuddenly be found to fucceed to
them. And I freely acknowledge that I think it a
ftrong argument, and one which, under other circumftances, it would have been very adventurous, and
perhaps very prepofterous, to controvert. But firmly
perfuaded as I am that the falvation of the country
and of Europe depends, not only upon our fuc ,
but upon our perfeverance in the war; and that time
is at leaft as neceffary as force itfelf, to coerce the in-
fatuated people againft whom we wage it; I am forry
to fee the efforts of the kingdom made fo furious and
violent, and our ftrength and refources exerted and
exhaufted with fo little forefight or difcretion, as to
leave us no alternative between immediate triumph
and immediate ruin. And this I fay, Sir, indepen-
dently of the abfurdity and ignorance with which
thefe efforts have been directed, and which have naturally caufed them to mifcarry in fo many places.

The force of France has always been proportioned to
the vigour of the attack made upon her, and has never been greater than it, becaufe it required the danger to create the fpirit, and the exigency to furnifh
the means of refiftance. If France had been attacked
by us at fea only, fhe would have beheld St. Do-
mingo, Martinico, Gaudaloupe, the Mauritius, the
Ifle

Ifle of Bourbon, and all her Indian poffeffions in either world, furrender one by one, with a careleffnefs and indifference, of which it is not eafy to form an idea, without having read the books, and obferved the effect of the books, circulated fo long at Paris, by the Briffotine party in particular; and without having witneffed the enthufiafm with which, even before the gates of the Hotel de Maffiac, " *périffent les colonies,*" had been echoed upon every occafion, where there had been a queftion of commerce or colonization, in oppofition to Republicanifm or war. But fuppofing me to over-rate the indifference with which thefe loffes might have been received at Paris, I fhall not, I apprehend, be contradicted, when I affert that they could not have caufed all the fenfation there, nor all the alarm, nor all the indignation which we have feen excited by dangers nearer home, and by the fiege of towns, in which we have preferred to take a part, to fo many richer and more eafy acquifitions. Tobago loft occafioned fcarce a murmur; but the unhappy attempt againft Dunkirk put all France into a ftate of requifition, and embodied the very mafs of the people in one innumerable militia.—The whole plan of the war, I confefs, appears to me to have been miftaken, defective, and abfurd. If if was thought poffible to frighten France, as it appeared to M. Mallet du Pan, and the royalifts, we ought to have declared, or according to a more favourite fyftem of the Cabinet, to have threatened at leaft, when Auftria and Pruffia coalefced, and to have become parties

to

to the declaration of Pilnitz. The common declaration of all Europe might perhaps at that time have intimidated France, but the Courts came fo flowly into the confederation, and dropped fo childifhly and fo timidly one after another into the fcheme, that whatever effect might have been hoped from terror or aftonifhment, was now entirely forfeited and paft. If it was thought poffible to crufh France by one general effort, and that Auftrians, Pruffians, Spaniards and Piedmontefe, by a common and concerted irruption, difregarding fuch paltry obftacles as the Rhine, the Alps, and the Pyrenees, and the Alps and Pyrenees of Vauban in particular, might unite their forces at the capital, as it appeared to M. de Bouillé and the wives of the emigrants; then the Britifh Fleet was " *hors de combat,*" and the Maréfchal de Freytag became a perfonage of more importance than my Lord Howe, my Lord Hood, and all their Admirals! If this fyftem had been adopted, or rather confided in, for I am afraid it was never defpaired of intirely, before experience had begot a ftill worfe kind of defpair, if this fyftem had been trufted to, the fubfidies to Sardinia, Heffe, Hanover, &c. &c. would not have been half fo abfurd, becaufe they would naturally have derived from the abfurd fyftem which had been adopted; but when that fyftem was adopted, which for the fake of being intelligible, I call a fyftem, and it was determined to carry on hoftilities every where, without carrying war any where; when it was agreed to fritter and dribble away the force of the kingdom

without

without any fixed object or defign, and to puzzle if we could not frighten France, with the immenfity and the multiplicity of our objects, when with two hundred and eighty veffels of war, it was determined to do nothing by fea, and in fpite of nature, policy, and experience, to attempt every thing by land; I fay, when thefe views were adopted, which feemed, no doubt, fo wife and fo eafy to my Lord Chatham, and fo wife and fo natural to the Duke of Richmond, when thefe views were adopted, and we had troops or commiffioners in every camp, not to fpeak of the criminal abfurdity of having a camp of our own, when all thefe things were evident, it feemed evident alfo, that the prodigality of the war, was not only accidental or negligent, but defigned and acceffory to other plans and defigns, and the fate of Europe wilfully and deliberately fet upon one defperate caft. This no doubt encouraged the enemy as much as it difcouraged the nation; and difgufted the nation by its juft apprehenfions, as much as it irritated the ene-my by its juft contempt, and by the partial but in-effectual impreffions which were fo ufelefsly made upon its territory.

Now, Sir, the object of the war, which is as dif-ferent from its caufe, as its caufe is from the circum-ftances thatn eceffitated its declaration, is, in my opi-nion, neither more nor lefs, than to repulfe the French within their own territory while they are mad, and having cured them of their madnefs, or awaited the

abatement

abatement of the fit, to fend every man home to his particular employment and profeſſion, and to extinguiſh the principle that every man is a foldier, and every field common. Wherever theſe doctrines are believed or enforced, there can be no fecurity for any neighbouring State, for either it muft be conquered and overrun, or it muft grow mad too, in order to be able to refift by the fame numbers and exertions. A ftanding army fet up in one kingdom has forced all the States of Europe to maintain ftanding armies, and a ftanding revolution will neceſſitate ftanding revolutions. France is juſt now powerful becaufe ſhe is ruined, we are weak becaufe we fear to be ruined ; but the fame crimes would enable us to difplay the fame vigour, and rather than be deſtroyed by France, it is probable we ſhould declare the property and lives of the kingdom in a ftate of requifition too. I have ftated this becaufe it was our duty and intereft to ſuffer France to crumble by her own rottenneſs, to oppofe her only fo much and no more, as her own particular violence and ambition ſhould require from us, to have aſſifted the royaliſts and the federaliſts too, and every fect or party, that divided or oppofed the Convention, and diminiſhed the central ftrength and authority of Paris ; and to have neither declared nor betrayed any predilection for any form of her difputable Government, much lefs to have pledged ourfelves in favour of the moſt defperate of all ; and to have aſſerted in our Manifefto as a fact, what every individual in that country knew

to

to be a falfehood, the operation of which they would inftantly conclude to be intended to deceive and to blind another country than their own. The war ought. to have been confidered as fecondary and auxiliary to the infurrections, and no counter-revolution to have been looked for except from the experience of their own mifery and crimes, and from their own re-pentance and remorfe.

The Jacobins, who one would imagine were the the only ftatefmen in Europe, inftead of being dif-mayed with the formidable but ill-connected force which menaced them, were well pleafed at an idle ap-pearance, which lent them real ftrength and refources, and enabled them to unite almoft every defcription of perfons in the caufe of the capital, which it was now eafy to confound with that of the nation; their violence kept pace with the threats of the in-vader, and their force redoubled even with his fuc-ceffes; they were able to confifcate and to plunder, to confine, to try, to execute, and to grow rich and terrible together, in proportion as he advanced into their territory or triumphed over their volunteers. They knew to turn every misfortune into an advan-tage, and gathered ftrength from every defeat; they had nothing to apprehend in particular from any one quarter of the war, and they derived a general and univerfal power and augmentation, from every particu-lar lofs or accident which happened to them in any. Such were the confequences of the mode adopted of

carrying

carrying on the war. But if the war had been conducted fastidiously, (if I may use such an expreffion)
if Great-Britain in particular had precifely proportioned her efforts to the efforts of France, obferving
always that fuperiority in each department of it
which was necessary to infure fuccefs; the long and
diftant profpect would have damped and obfcured
the fanguine vifion of the Convention; it would have
carried defpair into its own bofom, and given it no
pretence, no opportunity to animate and exalt the
paffions of the people; it would have feen many years
of hoftility and danger hanging over it, and its
object would have become faint and indiftinct from
the remotenefs and contingency of its completion.
It would have feen its ports blockaded, its commerce
ruined, its fupplies cut off, its provifions intercepted,
perhaps its Fleets attacked and beaten; ftill Great-
Britain would fcarce have perceived fhe was at war;
her expences would have been moderate, and her
commerce might have encreafed from the encreafe of
her maritime poffeffions, from the complete command of the Levant trade; and even of the Baltic,
if fhe had thought proper to negociate before the
actual commencement of hoftilities; and what, in my
mind, is more valuable than any other confideration,
fhe might have remained at the end of the war the umpire and arbitrefs of Europe, inftead of an interefted
and exhaufted party in the quarrel, and poffibly inftead
of being compelled to accept the terms of pacification,

tion, from another power, who may difcover an Oc-
zakow in the Weft-Indies, or the Mediterranean.

From what I have faid, my dear Sir, you will eafily underftand that my objection to treating (though
I would not in any cafe treat with thefe who had
been perfonally inftrumental in the public crimes) is
not becaufe France is republican, but becaufe fhe is
revolutionary, it is not the form of her government,
but the principle of her civil union, (if it may ftill be
called fo) which forms an eternal barrier to peace, becaufe it is incompatible with the confidence or fecurity
of furrounding States. The queftion, therefore, will
be this, are we to reduce or to exterminate this people
with whom we cannot treat, before we can lay down
our arms, and return to our fields and manufactures?
Or at what point of conqueft and fuccefs will it be
fafe to fufpend our hoftilities? I had rather his Majefty's fervants would condefcend to anfwer this important queftion, than attempt it for myfelf; but it
appears to me, Sir, that we need not to carry on an
eternal or indefinite warfare, notwithftanding the impoffibility of treating. It is, I think, pretty much
with nations as it is with individuals, in whom it is
impoffible to confide; a pledge or a depofit is as valuable and as fafe from the hands of a knave, as from
thofe of a man of honour, and the poffeffion of towns
and iflands, of territories and of commerce, may
oubtle be as good a fecurity for obferving the

K terms

terms of a contract, as the oath of a King, or the fignature of an Ambaſſador. In the ſtrict caſe of the
uti-poſſidetis I can ſee no occaſion for any treaty at all,
and I am convinced that a treaty is an uſeleſs formality. I make war to obtain poſſeſſion of Calais, I take
Calais and no one endeavours to retake it; I might
ſurely reſt upon my arms in ſuch a caſe, and might
diſpenſe too with a treaty, becauſe no treaty could
ever make out a title, or convey it to me by any better or ſafer tenure than my own ſuperiority.

He who looks for any other treaty than this, under
any event, or any other ſecurity from the phyſical
preponderance of France, than our own ſtrength and
thoſe moral reſources, which the ſpirit, the induſtry,
and the virtues of our nation, have hitherto ſupplied
to combat in this unequal field; is blind to that un-
conquerable malice and envy, with which our little
iſland is regarded by that vain and diſappointed people, to that ſpirit of ambition and revenge, to thoſe
idle boaſts of "*delenda eſt Carthago*," which have been
echoed from the impure mouth of Barrére and his
colleagues, to every ſea and every mountain that en-
circles France; and what is more, which have been
caught up and prolonged in diſtant realms, by the
very exiles and fugitives of France; who in the
wreck of all their fortunes, amidſt the maſſacres of
their friends and companions, amidſt regicide and
ſacrilege, and univerſal miſery, ſeem to regret nothing

thing in banifhment or poverty fo much as the opportunity they have loft of conquering their hofts
and benefactors.

If there be any man in this kingdom fo abfurd as
to expect from the reftoration of the French monarchy, any firm alliance, or any fenfe or memory of
obligation from France, he knows little of nations in
general, and nothing, I think, of that nation in particular. If we are really to make the war for this
end, we are fighting for thofe who are already, I fear,
ungrateful, and will add ingratitude to all the vices
and crimes that have plunged them in fo many misfortunes. To his Majefty's Minifters I can only addrefs my earneft prayer, that they would be pleafed,
at laft, to explain " the real grounds of the war," in
a precife and unequivocal manner, let them conduct
it how they will ; for almoft any war is better than a
fhameful, an infincere, and an infecure pacification ;
let us know what we bleed for, and how long we are
to bleed ; remove this cloud from our eyes, *ι δι φατι
και ολισσον.* It is indifferent to me whether Jupiter dif-
perfes the mift by the help of Mr. Bowles or of another Manifefto.

But if it fhould be judged imprudent in his Majefty's fervants, who, notwithftanding the calumnies
of their enemies, feem determined to treat at one
time or other, and to treat with Danton rather than

not

not to treat at all ; if it is judged imprudent in thofe who chofe to mif-tranflate Lord Auckland, rather than to avow him, to preclude themfelves, by any previous engagement or explanation refpecting the caufes or objects of the war, from concluding the peace under any other event or circumftance than thofe which they had ftipulated and forefeen ; then, it will be proper to change the queftion, and to intreat, that his Majefty's Minifters will be pleafed to acquaint us (a piece of information, I confefs, I expected when I heard of the treaty concluded in the camp of the King of Pruffia, under the aufpices of my Lord Yarmouth) whether the republic is in any cafe to be treated with, and to be acknowledged under any condition ? And as we cannot learn at what point of fuccefs it may be poffible to paufe with fecurity, we may demand without much danger, I imagine, what degree of misfortune, ill-conduct, abfurdity, and difhonour, will make it appear neceffary to negociate, or at leaft to fufpend hoftilities ? but perhaps they will have no judges but experience itfelf of the period beyond which it will be impoffible to confide to them any longer the conduct of the war ?

In my own opinion, to declare we will not treat with the republic, is as unwife and as unjuft, as to infift upon the reftoration of any form of government, whether republic, defpotifm, or conftitution ; I fhould be willing to treat with either, as foon as we can

have

have any fecurity for the obfervance of the ftipulations of peace. Difarm, fend back your labourers, your peafants, to their farms; refcind your decrees of general requifition; thefe are the firft articles of any treaty; whoever is able to promife and to perform thefe ftipulations, is Government enough to treat with, becaufe it is Government enough to afford fecurity to the parties in the contract; and if we refufe to treat, whenever we can treat with this fecurity, it appears to me that the objects of the war are more extenfive than the caufes, and that we are fighting for fomething elfe befides our own fafety and the tranquillity of Europe.

But, believe me, my dear Sir, that this fatisfaction, which I implore for the nation, is not merely to gratify its curiofity, nor to extinguifh any vain doubts, or unreafonable fufpicions; when that corrupt agreement took place, between the Court and the Minifters, by which the ftrength and popularity of reform were abandoned for the power of prodigality, and the means of impunity: by which the Court, with true papal cunning, exchanged its bull of indulgencies for an undifturbed and fecurer term in its own luxury and uncleannefs; when this union and alliance became known by its effects, and the war was jointly declared againft the French and the Reformers, againft the Convention and the prefs, it was natural, at leaft during fo much noife and clamour, that it fhould diftract and perplex the under-

K 3   ftanding

ftanding of the people; and accordingly we found, that fome of them very early confidered the war as the war of the Court, and dreaded the fucceffes of our arms, as an acceffion of power to this domeftic enemy, whom they defpifed, and dreaded, and de tefted infinitely more than the foreign. There were others, who openly defired the fuccefs of the French arms, which they thought could alone protect us againft the' formidable league, which not only ex-cluded reform, but threatened the remains of liberty and independence: and who would have feen the Convention triumph with exultation, as the means of punifhing, or abolifhing the Court. I cannot help ftopping in this place, to remark to you the fquea-mifhnefs and coquetry of the Court upon this occa-fion, which affected to pout and to be vaftly fur-prized and affronted, that the people fhould defpife or deteft it as much as the Jacobins; juft as if tho ferocious vices were entitled to all our hatred and contempt, and we fhould have no refentments left for the bafe and degrading; as if the bold and hardy character of crimes were alone the caufe of horror, and we were to feel no indignation at meannefs, fraud, fervility, avarice, extortion, and oppreffion!

It is certain however, that the people, upon their fide, very foon began to apprehend, that victories would only procure to their old enemy a new leafe and perpetuity in its abufes, and to confider the Prince. of Saxe-Cobourg, as fighting the battles of Lord Chamberlains

Chamberlains and Lords of the Bed-chamber, inftead of thofe of Europe and of mankind; an opinion
the more dangerous, as, joined to the perfecution of
the bookfellers, it had introduced a real fchifm into
the kingdom, which could not have been otherwife
than united, if the Government had explained all
the danger which threatened us, and left the fentiments of horror and antipathy it defired us to feel,
to the free workings of our own underftanding. But
feeling its own weaknefs, from the unpopularity
of its new ally, it was always afraid to confefs
the whole of the danger; till the ill conduct and
mifcarriages of the war, by encreafing this fear,
have at laft forced its weaknefs into the abominable
impofition, to which it has condefcended, of repre-
fenting the generality of the enemy as difpofed to
counter-revolution and monarchy : Thus is a fyftem
of fraud, diffimulation, perfidy, and dilhonour, naturally engrafted upon a treaty, in which public virtue
and public utility were made to give way to a mean
and contemptible policy, unworthy the Viziers and
eunuchs of an Eaftern Seraglio, and by which the
impunity of Minifters was purchafed, by prolonging
the wrongs and miferies of the people.

Now, Sir, nothing can be more important than to
do away this fatal impreffion; the reduction of the
Civil Lift, and the reform of the Parliament, would,
doubtlefs, be the moft effectual meafures which could
be purfued for this defirable purpofe : but an explicit

K 4   declaration

declaration from authority of the true fituation of the
kingdom, of the views entertained by Government,
of the profpects of peace, or of the term of hoftilities, could not be without a ftrong and beneficial
effect for the prefent; and I fincerely indulg e the
hope of feeing the next *State Paper*, whether diftinguifhed by the appellation of Speech or Manifefto,
that fhall be dated from Weftminfter or St. James's,
conceived in a more manly and more honourable ftrain,
polluted by no craft or diffimulation, advancing no
falfehoods, no equivocal facts nor opinions, but addreffed to the plain fenfe and magnanimity of the nation, worthy of it, and of him who is to fpeak to it.

But though from the paft conduct, and actual difpofition of the King's fervants, I cannot entertain
any fanguine expectation of finding them inclined to
diminifh corruption, or to concur with thofe who
demand a greater fecurity for the freedom and independency of the Houfe of Commons; whether they
feek it by new experiments, or would have recourfe
for it to ancient and approved remedies, I fhould
blame myfelf exceedingly, were I to fupprefs the
aftonifhment and concern I feel at the imbecility and
the obftinacy of thofe perverfe or perfidious councils, which have not only refufed redrefs to the
people, but dared to multiply grievances, and to ac-
cumulate the caufes of complaint. I confefs, Sir, I
doubt whether the nurfery for young ftatefmen will
ever repay to the nation all the charges of this new and

delicate

delicate attention; and I entertain some fears left they should escape out of it too soon, notwithstanding the mess of porridge which might otherwise tempt them to sojourn, because so many others of the sons of the prophets may be desirous to partake of it in their turn; in truth I fear that some of them may prove truant, and be discovered to be Ambassadors and Plenipotentiáries at foreign Courts, before, in spite of their political accomplishments, the law will allow them to be at age of discretion. I protest, Sir, I entertain this apprehension, not from want of respect to any of the young gentlemen, who are actually charged with his Majesty's procuration to so many of the Sovereigns Europe; but because I think the nation may be dishonoured by it. If other nations are not insulted, by making their Courts, the nursery of our infant-politicians I think our own nation dishonoured by it, not because these young men do not acquit themselves, at least as well as might be expected in their task, but because it inclines all Europe to believe the *calumnies* that are vomitted against our Constitution, and to suspect that every employment, every department of the State is usurped by the tyranny and injustice of aristocracy and connexion!

To return from grievances to those who sweat and suffer under all, who feed these nurseries, and pay these baby embassies,—to the people: is it wise, for I speak not of its honesty, to provoke and exasperate, and insult it, at a time when so much industry and artifice

have

have been employed to difguft it with the Conftitution all together? If the people were gratified in half
its juft and reafonable defires, it would be out of the
power of agitators and reformers to make it an inftrument to extort unjuft or unreafonable conceffions.
But when the people is once made to demand, he
who can cry the loudeft, and demands the moft, appears its true and only friend; it favours the violent,
and confides only in the enthufiaftic and the head-
ftrong. We begin by demanding its rights; another demands exemptions or favours; a third flat-
ters its paffions and prejudices, and a fourth offers
majefty, and proclaims the fovereignty of the people.
All thefe men have their turn, but the wickedeft and
moft defperate is always the laft; Petion fucceeds
to La Fayette, Marat to Petion; and after Marat
comes a Robefpierre, a Danton, or a Barrere. Let us
not prefume too far upon the character and virtues of
the country; all crowds are dangerous, all affemblies
cruel. Were we to undergo in England a violent
reform, or to depute a National Convention, I am
not convinced that we fhould legiflate with much
more wifdom or juftice than we have feen in France;
though I think we fhould execute, or even violate our
laws, with more regard to humanity, to mercy, and
to nature. We fhould no doubt have our plunde-
rers and levellers, but perhaps affaffins and murderers
would be more uncommon; we fhould have pro-
fcriptions, though we might efcape maffacres; and
we might be violent, without being deliberately
cruel;

cruel; even punifhment and revenge itfelf might di-
veft themfelves amongft us of fome of their French
ferocity, fome of their adventitious refinement and
horror. But this is all that I dare indulge my national
vanity to hope for in fuch a ferment and convulfion of
men's minds, during the fhock of authorities, the
filence of law, and the fubverfion of every rule and
principle of human fociety.   Thofe who would
plunge us into this crifis, whether they be ftatefmen
or the enemies of ftates, whether they be the followers
of Mr. Pitt or of Mr. Paine, are, in my mind, the
moft deliberate incendiaries; and I am forry to fay,
that in fuch a complicity of crime, I can only diftinguifh, in favour of thofe who may have overftepped
in a juft caufe, againft thofe who fhall have been unjuft and tyrannical frem the beginning.

If therefore you, my dear Sir, remain as thoroughly
convinced, as you appeared to be a few weeks fince,
of the impolicy and injuftice of the King's Minifters
and the majority of the Houfe of Commons, in re-
fufing fatisfaction to the people upon this fubject :
Of the danger of trifling with the wifhes and the
complaints of a free and powerful nation; of the
crime and flagitioufnefs of driving the country to
defpair, and forcing men to have recourfe to meafures, which defpair alone can juftify : If you remain convinced of the wickednefs of having engaged
us in a continental war, and the folly and incapacity
with which that war has been conducted; of the
fhameful

fhameful and inexplicable inactivity of our fleets, of the difhonour attending our mifcarriages before Martique and Guadaloupe; of the neglect and want of forefight at Toulon, to which I have fince been forced to add a heavier charge, and of the univerfal ill conduct of the Admiralty-Board; of the ignorance, errors, and treachery, which caufed the mifcarriage of the Duke of York before Dunkirk, the defeat of the Feldt Marefchal de Freytag, and of General Clairfait, the raifing the fiege of Maubeuge, and the repaffing of the Sambre, which inverted or ruined all the plans of the campaign, and fowed the fruitful feeds of difcord amongft the combined armies; of the conceit, impertinence, and abftract abfurdity, of impofing that meafure upon his Royal Highnefs and the allies; if, in fhort, you are convinced, as I have reafon to believe, that we can expect nothing good, either at home or abroad, from his Majefty's Minifters; that they act without plan or forefight, without concert or principle; that they have contrived to render abfolutely ineffectual, and paralytic, all our efforts by fea, and unfortunate all our expeditions at land; that they have difhonoured our arms, for I can never repeat it too often, upon that element, where we never poffeffed, no Sir, nor any nation, nor any confederacy of nations, ever poffeffed fo great and decided fuperiority over the enemy; that they have expofed the Britifh name to reproach and ignominy, by the comparifon which muft be made by every Court in Europe, between the glorious victories we obtained in the laft war, when we combated

againft

againſt France, and againſt all the world, and our late atchievements, now that we combat againſt France alone, with all the world on our ſide, now when we want nothing but an enemy, and then when we could find nothing that was not an enemy ; if you are convinced, in ſhort, that the King's ſervants poſſeſs neither the talents to give us glory or ſucceſs abroad, nor the virtue to grant us peace and juſtice at home, you will find yourſelf, like me, unable to give them your confidence, and you will juſt give them that degree of ſupport, which will appear to you to be neceſſary to hinder their adverſaries from ſeizing the helm of affairs, and making an infamous peace with our enemies ; you will ſupport them upon that principle which induced the woman of Syracuſe to pray for the life of Dionyſius the tyrant, from the greater apprehenſion ſhe' entertained of his ſucceſſors ; you will neither approve nor applaud their meaſures, nor even join in the formality of an addreſs ; you will ſuſpect, you will watch, you will reſtrain the Adminiſtration; you will awe, you will intimidate, you will ſilence the ambition, the madneſs of the Oppoſition ; you will repreſent the anxiety and ſuſpence that agitate the nation, and the imminent hazards which reſult, from its being unable to place its confidence, or entruſt its complaints to any known or reſponſible party in the kingdom ; you will impreſs Miniſters with the neceſſity of yielding to the remonſtrances of the people, of avoiding inſurrections by juſt conceſſion and diſappointing revolutions, by rational re-

form ;

form; you will inculcate the hatred and contempt of corrupt placemen and courtiers, and diftinguifh the pure and generous loyalty of Britons to their King, from the bafe crouching of flaves to the mandarins and fatrapes of St. James's; you will imprefs even Minifters themfelves with the prudence and the neceffity (you will not, perhaps, think it incumbent upon you to talk to them of the duty or the virtue) of difbanding thofe mercenary troops, which are their own tyrants, as well as the tyrants and the famifhers of the people; of the advantage and popularity of reducing finecures ˙and diminifhing the Civil Lift, before they venture to levy that enormous mafs of frefh taxes and impofitions, which their prodigal and abfurd mifmanagement of the war has made neceffary, and which cannot be diffembled or palliated by loans, or by an averfion, a delay, or an impoffibility to fund them. You will do what is in your power, and more is in no man's power, to bring them to a fenfe of policy and of fear, the only impreffion under which it is reafonable to expect from them either wifdom or juftice, and you will be ready to ftand forth the champion of the people's juft rights, and to difappoint the ambition of both factions, the minifterial and the revolutionary !

You who are fo well acquainted with my fentiments upon thefe fubjects, will not be inclined to fufpect, from any thing that I have faid, that I lean beyond a juft bias towards the reprefentative fyftem;

tem ; but as I am anonymous to nearly all the world but yourfelf, it is neceffary for me, or at leaft prudent, to give my political creed and confeffion with regard to it; and 1 fhall do it with fincerity, perhaps with too much fimplicity. I think then no fyftem fo true, fo beautiful, fo natural, or fo fublime, in theory ; and I am convinced, that republics upon this principle, muft be the favourite governments of all enlightened minds, and the idols of every generous fpirit, I mean till they have been tried ; for in the practice and experiment they are found to fail miferably, and to depart widely from their promife and expectation ; it is the experience of the ill, and unftable government of republics that has made any man of fenfe or fpirit fubmit, or defire to live under monarchies ; now, unfortunately, the people who cannot read nor reafon, and have no experience but their own, unacquainted with hiftory, and ftrangers to the States and Governments around them, know of no bad or unftable Government but their own ; born under monarchy, they attribute to it the evils infeparable from human focieties ; and think, that if they could get rid of a particular form of Government and of a King, they fhould be freed alfo from the hardfhips they fuffer and the burthens they endure. If a people be oppreffed and unhappy under a republican form of government, which is more likely than under the monarchical, becaufe there rarely exifts a great degree of civil liberty under this regimen (and political liberty is of fmall comparative

importance

importance to the mafs of fociety,) the fame principle will operate under a different form, for they will think that by getting rid of a fenate or of a council, or by accepting a King, they fhall be difcharged from their contributions, and that their grievances will be inftantly redreffed.—The people therefore defire a change, becaufe from a change they.expect every thing : Uncertain of the future, weary of the paft, and impatient of the prefent, they indulge the hope and delufive dream of a fanguine imagination, and fatigued, and exhaufted with their known grievances willingly commit themfelves with confidence and ardor to whatever is new and untried. Of the reprefentative fyftem therefore, which is theoretically fo beautiful, I entertain this.opinion, that it is calculated peculiarly to feduce the imagination, and to biafs the judgment, of thofe perfons, efpecially, who have neither leifure nor opportunity to confider it when reduced to its action and experiment as a Government ; and I think it more eafy to make the mafs of a people difcontented with the monarchical inftitution, from the hope and beauty of the reprefentative, than it is *vice verfa* to difguft republican States with their form of Government, and to induce amongft them a defire and eagernefs after the monarchical fyftem. For this reafon too, I think it abfurd. and dangerous in the extreme, in the King's fervants to break their faith, and trifle with the people upon fuch delufive and flattering ground.—As to the reprefentative part of our own Conftitution, I am free to confefs, that I

think

think all the liberty, all the bleſſings we either enjoy, or
have enjoyed, or have a right to look for, have been,
and muſt be, derived implicitly from this branch of
our legiſlature, and muſt depend for their ſecurity
and duration upon its independence and virtue;
and this ſentiment would make me groan over the
corruption and depravity of the Houſe of Commons, while the vices of the Court, and the indolence and vanity of the Houſe of Lords, could ſcarce
excite any ſenſation in my breaſt but that of ſcorn or
faſtidious pity, or perhaps involuntary diſguſt.

Neither am I at all clear, that the repreſentative
ſyſtem could long ſubſiſt in its vigour or purity in
any State, where it was not reſtrained and coereed
by ſome other independent and integral body; and
I am far from being ſatisfied, with the experience
which is ſaid to be furniſhed us in the American
form of Government.—In France we have found the
Monarch was unable to controul it, but I think this
inſtance proves very little againſt it, juſt as the
former proves very little in its favour; for both, in
my opinion, are matters of circumſtance, which have
never been fairly brought to experiment or trial.
Had Louis the ſixteenth, enjoyed, or had Waſhing-
ton not enjoyed the confidence of their reſpective
countries, I think it very poſſible, that the direct
contrary inference might now have been concluded
from each of theſe examples; that the French Conſtitution might have yet ſtood, and the American

L   have

have given way. So little do I feel myself entitled
to appeal to either of thefe queftionable and imperfect authorities. Yet I think from a remoter experience and analogy, it is more probable that the reprefentative fyftem fhould exift, under the mild and
gradual compreffion or reaction of a fenate, than
under the enormous weight and difparity of a throne.
not only on account of the hatred and danger of Courts,
but becaufe between a King and a people, there is a
fudden and a mighty difproportion, and an intermediate political body feems to be abfolutely neceffary
to connect them together, if a people would have
any liberty, or a King any fecurity at all. A people
too may refift a fenate, and make a hundred partial
revolutions without totally overthrowing or fubvert-
ing the fyftem of Government, becaufe fome of that
body will remain, and the reft may be fupplied ; and
of thofe that remain, the majority will have probably
become popular, by adopting the prevailing fentiments of the times, and thereby be able to damp or
to intercept the blow, before it crufhes or annihilates
the order.—Individuals may perifh, but the political
body may remain, be invigorated or renewed, which
can fcarce happen for the moft evident reafons, in the
cafe of a violent revolution, in monarchical Governments.

The defire of change fo natural therefore to every
people, (for the lot of every people is, I fear,
unhappy, and certainly is not fo happy as it always
feems

feems poffible to make it) appears to me to be more dangerous in monarchical ftates, than in republics of any defcription : and there is great room to apprehend that it is now exceedingly ftrong in our own, and that it will acquire force, and break out with irrefiftible fury as foon as the fear of anarchy and maffacre fhall have evaporated, or as foon as any poffible fuccefs or advantage fhould attend the arms of France, or the French Revolution become at all eftablifhod upon any firm or apparent bafis. It is then, my dear Sir, I think peculiarly to be defired, at this awful and important crifis, that the people fhould have no wanton or unneceffary caufe of complaint; and that the love of change, and the temptation to change, fhould be as little encouraged or encreafed as is poffible. And I think befides, that Minifters and Courts would act wifely to confult not only the interefts and the rights, but the affections and the paffions of the people, at a time when fo many arts and delufions are practifed to inflame them. But the vanity and ambition of fome men caufes them to defire and prefer turbulent times, in which they flatter themfelves they fhall be able always to bear fway, and makes them confide in being received at any time as chiefs and heroes by the partizans of every revolution.

This was the precife cafe of the Minifter Neckar, and may be the cafe of Minifters as vain and lefs honeft than Neckar, if they will not take warning by

his

his example, to extinguifh juft complaints as faft as they arife, rather than to encourage and provoke them, delaying the remedy, and fomenting the dif-eafe, till fuch critical and dangerous periods, as they expect, will make the relief more valued, and them-felves more popular and powerful for affording it. But thefe courfes are the moft dangerous, as well as the moft wicked they can purfue; for in fuch mo-ments of heat and fermentation, the people is not contented with the redrefs of its grievances. It is fenfible of its force, as well as of its wrongs; and as it attributes every conceffion on the part of its op-preffors to the effect of their fears and apprehenfions, it determines to encreafe or to continue the impref-fion, which is fo favourable to its own interefts and paffions. In fuch a moment, thofe who demand are more popular than thofe who grant; and he that menaces is more powerful than him that concedes. The people enjoys a triumph as often as it obtains redrefs, and had rather conquer its rights than re-ceive them.

If the people had been indulged at firft with that temperate Reform which they wanted, and which it is fo bafe and fo indecent to refufe them, the Mini-fter, it is true, would not have derived a dangerous, but he would have gained a folid and a juft populari-ty: as there would have been neither anxiety nor peril, fo there would have been neither intemperance nor ex-ceffive exultation. It is to be apprehended it cannot

now

now be granted without the people's being induced to believe they owe it to the fears and pufillanimity of Minifters or of Parliament; and that they will look upon it rather as a triumph that they have won, than a right reftored, or a benefit conferred upon them. The Minifter and his rival may run a race for this popularity, but the wife and honeft, will fee that it is extorted from both, and the people will not long remain the dupes of the competition. I think it neceffary, therefore, that the party I have fpoken of fhould be formed fpeedily, not only to procure a Reform from the unwilling juftice of both fides of the Houfe, but to confer it with any grace or fafety upon the people: and I am the more defirous to fee the foundation at leaft laid, of fuch a party, becaufe I think its very appearance might check the impatience and indignation of the people, and perfuade them to expect the reafonable gratification of their wifhes by calm and temperate means, and from hands at which they would be content to receive it; which it is much to be apprehended they would not, in the prefent irritable difpofition of their minds, be inclined to do from fuch as have already bafely and impudently violated their promifes and engagements with regard to it, or from fuch as have funk into contempt and difcredit, from the profligate oppofition they have given to meafures of public neceffity, and fallen fo low, both in number and eftimation, as to move no fentiments but thofe of ridicule, averfion, or pity.

That

That a third party *will* arife to extort this benefit, and to take the ambitious merit of having conferred it upon the people, appears to me fo plain, and fo evident, that my only concern, and my only ap-prehenfion, is with regard to the purity, the in-dependence, and the integrity of its compofition. That the people will finally acquire the benefit I have no doubt; and therefore I am exceedingly anxious that it fhould acknowledge the obligation, *where it is fafe for it to be grateful.* For this reafon I anxioufly wifh, that the body who fhall procure it for them, and prefent it to them, were fo compofed that it might embrace the untainted part of the actual authorities, and men of honour, and of abilities, and of property, of every party and defcription; and it is for this rea-fon that I fear, left from the overfight or the too great caution of fuch perfons, it fhould be formed out of the bold and bad men, who have prefided in clubs and affemblies, or led our mutinous deputations of Englifh to the bar of the French Convention, or cir-culated its wild theories and inflammatory manifeftos amongft the people.; and left the people, either in the eagernefs to obtain this benefit, or in gratitude for it, fhould throw itfelf into the arms of thefe tur-bulent and unprincipled men, in whofe hands it will prefently become a dangerous inftrument to level every rank, introduce new and deftrnctive princi-ples of property, and lay the admired fabric of our Conftitution lower than the throne of Louis the Six-teenth.

In

In calling upon Mr. Fox to prefide over fuch a party, I had entertained the double view of gaining a leader of his power, experience, and abilities on the fide of honeft and conftitutional reform ; and of cutting off the hope and expectation of the fpeculative and the diffaffected of every fect and party, who evidently courted him, and looked up to him, as one that was foon to take the command and direction of them. His conduct at that time caufed me extreme uneafinefs ; and I cannot repent of the pains I have taken, and the inducements I have held out to recall him from a precipice, fo dangerous to himfelf and to his country. I had confidence befides in the virtues of his mind, and I was in hopes to make them combat with me, againft the impetuofity of his paffions, the rancour of his difappointment, and the violence of his ambition. I may not perhaps have failed fo entirely in my attempt, as the imperfect fuccefs of it may at firft fight induce you to imagine; from my own motives, and from the honeft rewards I held out to him, I had reafon, no doubt, to hope a better and more entire converfion.

Diis aliter vifum eft.

But whatever may be your opinions or prejudices with regard to this extraordinary perfonage, you will allow, I am fure, that he has always acted an important character upon our political theatre; and that it would be unwife, if it were not ungrateful to leave him out in any new caft of the parts. His abilities, .

lities, his vigour of mind, his comprehenfive judgment, his experience, his eloquence, even his inor-
dinate ambition, are fo many arguments with me for
employing him wherever there is room for him, if
it were only *ne noceat* : but I confefs I think he may
yet render fervices to Greece, that may make his Per-
fian voyages be forgotten.

In taking leave of you, Sir, and my fubject together,
let me intreat of you, whenever you are inclined to canvafs thefe ideas, to recollect not only what I have written, but what I have faid to you, with regard to them.
I have written with as much freedom as I dare, having
no intention to become a martyr to any caufe; in converfation there is lefs danger ; and warmth and animation are more natural and becoming; in that refpect, what I have fupprefied in this Letter, will re-
ceive infinite advantage, if it is recollected and re-
peated by you ; and you will poffibly gain for me
fome profelytes, more than you fufpect, if you en-
force my principles with the grace and elocution
which belong almoft exclufively to yourfelf. For
the reft, your political conduct and opinions, as long
as they are confiftent and fincere, let them be *pour ou
coutre*, can neither encreafe nor diminifh the efteem
and affection, with which I am, my dear Sir,

&c. &c. &c.

London, Jan. 10, 1794.

F I N I S.